70
Years
of Miracles

Richard H. Harvey

©1977, 1992
Horizon House Publishers
All Rights Reserved
ISBN: 0–88965–101–9
HORIZON BOOKS
are published by Horizon House Publishers
3825 Hartzdale Drive, Camp Hill, Pennsylvania 17011
Printed in the United States of America

DEDICATION

To my wife:
  Whose deep faith in Christ, love for the Word and loyalty to me have been a bulwark of encouragement for more than 50 years of sharing the experiences of life. She never faltered or wanted to quit when the going was rough. She would say, "We must pray it through and win—we don't retreat!" When the rewards are handed out on that Great Day by our Lord, hers will be greater.

Contents

Foreword

Many of God's servants today believe that "miracles" were merely a sign God used to establish the early Church and give it credibility. They claim that our needs are not as great today and therefore God no longer performs miracles.

Dr. Richard Harvey will promptly refute that argument in the pages to follow. His story is not just of one miracle—it's of a series of miracles that extends over more than 70 years!

Having sat on several boards and in numerous board meetings with Dr. Harvey and having worked with him in church organization and Christian education over a period of nearly 20 years, I can attest to the unlimited dedication, fervor and energy he has given to win souls to Christ by whatever means and talent God has laid at his disposal.

And his fervor seems to have increased with age. Retirement only embarked him on a new direction of overseas evangelism requiring the greatest physical strain of his life at a time when most men are slowing down.

But that, too, is one of the miracles of God's grace. "As thy days, so shall thy strength be" (Deut. 33:25) was the promise of God to Israel. Richard Harvey appropriated it also and has turned what might otherwise have been a "slow death" retirement into the pinnacle of his career for God.

My late father, Mr. R.G. LeTourneau, world-renowned Christian businessman and inventor, would make a special effort to be in any service in which Dr. Harvey was speaking. "His enthusiasm for the gospel makes him my kind of man," Dad would say.

As you read this account of what God can do through a man willing to put his effort and enthusiasm into God's plan and program, my prayer is that this will inspire you to "go and do likewise" for the kingdom of Christ.

Richard H. LeTourneau, Ph.D.
President, LeTourneau College
Longview, Texas

Introduction

Y ou may not believe this story of my life, but it is all true. Many have said, "All this could not have happened to one person," but it did. The story could not be written before now, because it has taken a lifetime of integrity to back up its authenticity. The only purpose for the story being put into print is that some may come to believe and put their full trust in the living God.

My wife, who has shared 47 years of these experiences, would testify, "I have never known a dull moment, and have wished many times our life together were not quite so hectic."

"Haven't you colored it some?" some might ask. I would answer that every true picture has its color and every person seeing or experiencing a scene of action will describe it as he sees or remembers it. The coloring and tinting of the story will be according to his own background, but still it can all be true. That is why the Gospels of the New Testament are all different, but not contradictory.

For example, here is a story I would like to hear

7

some others describe, because many are alive who still remember the incident:

Back in the mid-forties our family was traveling to the state of Washington. I had been participating in the second Youth for Christ International Convention, which had been held at Medicine Lake, Minnesota. In order to help meet the traveling expenses for a family of six plus a friend, I accepted an invitation to preach Monday evening at the town of Tyler in Southwest Minnesota.

The pastor who had invited me decided to make the meeting a county-wide effort and invited all the Protestant churches to cooperate. Then the local committee secured the county fairground and chose the racetrack to stage the event. Their plan was to use the grandstand for seating and a flatbed truck furnished with a piano and five chairs for the platform.

When the service time arrived the grandstand was packed. In fact, the group assembled was bigger than the town's population! The service began with congregational singing and with special music provided by the local churches.

The meeting was just nicely in progress when mosquitoes invaded the place—swarms of them. They seemed to have come by the millions. Repellents appeared useless. The grandstand looked like a mass calisthenics class as the people tried in vain to chase away the harassing creatures that had so rudely invaded our service.

Some of the people began to leave and I saw that unless something happened fast I was going to lose my crowd. I arose from my chair on the flatbed, interrupted the song leader and with a sense of desperation cried into the microphone, "Everybody please stand up!" The crowd seemed pleased to respond. I raised my hands toward the starry sky and cried, "Oh God, get rid of these mosquitoes, now! Amen." Immediately there was a strong gust of wind and the mosquitoes were gone.

At the close of the message scores of people knelt in the dust of the racetrack and invited Christ into their lives. Many of the "town characters" received Jesus Christ that night.

What did I preach about? I don't recall. How would others describe the incident? I would like to hear them. The story is true, but everyone present would tell it differently. Each would relate it according to the context of his own experience and memory.

So it is with the story of my life. It is all true. I relate it to you now.

Richard H. Harvey

Miracles

My experience with miracles is that God never performs them for show or because people want to see them. They come in the normal experiences of life as a person is filling his line of duty and are necessary to that person's fully obeying God.

Probably many people today are like the contemporaries of Christ in that they are looking for a sign. To such seekers, God withholds such gratifications of the flesh.

As far as I can remember, no thought of a spectacle was involved when in my ministry God performed miracles. I was never trying to prove anything.

For example, I never did (and never would) attempt to cast out demons in public. God can take care of His own glory.

Thus, throughout my life I have refused to write the accounts of the miracles God performed. Now that I have reached my full span of 70 years, I record them for the glory of God, and for family posterity, and for those who will follow me in the ministry and also face difficult and impossible situations.

In God's providence, my life has been full of miracles. I did not seek them for their own sake (and surely it would be folly to do so), but these things really happened. They have been the Lord's doing and marvelous in our eyes.

But nevertheless, I here affirm, the greatest miracle of all takes place when a human being is born into God's kingdom and a life is transformed. That is the kind of miracle God sprinkles everywhere hearts are hungry. Thank God for miracles, yes, but thank Him much more for His Son, Jesus Christ. Most of all, I rejoice that because of Him, my name is written in the Book of Life.

Richard H. Harvey

Be thou strong therefore and show thyself a man, and keep the charge of the Lord thy God and walk in His ways.

1 Kings 2:2–3

1 My Dad!

"The Rock of Gibraltar" is the term many people used to describe my father. He was solid, dependable and unmovable when he felt sure he was right. As concerning me, his son, I was a special gift of God, a son born out of due time when my mother was supposed to be unable to have another child.

Thus, before my arrival my parents gave me wholly to God. My father was very strict in his discipline and somewhat puritanical in his younger years. (He grew more mellow as the years went by.) My mother was much more tolerant and permissive, always manifesting love and tenderness toward me.

This early experience will demonstrate their attitudes better than any I know.

When I was about six years old my parents were going to have a church party at the parsonage. (My father had entered the ministry the year I was born.) A party at our home was an unusual event because money was too scarce.

At the table the previous day my mother had asked, "Richard, what kind of cake would you like me to bake for the party tomorrow night?"

"May I have any kind I want?" I asked. When I learned I could, I promptly answered, "Angel food cake!"

"All right, angel food cake it will be." Really, that was unthinkable in those days because an angel food cake took so many eggs.

Then Father interjected, "Son, what kind of ice cream would you like?" Now this dates me, as there were then, as far as I know, only three kinds of ice cream: vanilla, chocolate and strawberry.

"Strawberry!" I quickly answered.

The day of the party arrived and of course I was very excited. It wasn't long until all of us children were engaged in rambunctious play and I was definitely too noisy to please my father. He came toward me, and drawing me aside said, "Richard, you'd better settle down or else." I had received some of my father's "or elses" and remember them yet. I settled down for a while, trying to be quiet in my chair. But soon I forgot and became involved with my friends.

Then I saw my father coming toward me again. My heart jumped with fear when he took me aside into the hall. "Richard, this is your last warning. If I have to speak to you again, upstairs you'll go and there will be no ice cream and no cake." He left me and I returned to the living room. I sat quietly in a corner for a while longer, but soon I forgot again.

Suddenly my father reappeared, grabbed me by

the arm, placed his hand over my mouth and carried me upstairs. "Now son, if there is any noise or crying that can be heard, I'll close the door and you will be in the dark." Then he tossed me on the bed. Into the pillow I sank my head, and I sobbed my heart out in misery and disappointment. Soon I heard the silverware on plates. I thought, "There goes my ice cream and cake!" I could hear all the merriment and knew very well what was going on.

Later, I learned my mother had wanted to save some of the refreshments for me, but my father wouldn't hear of it. "I told him there wouldn't be any," he had said and so there wasn't any!

Obedience and keeping one's word were very important to my parents, especially my father. One of his favorite quotations was, "Happy is the man that sweareth to his own hurt and changeth not." My father would frequently say, "Son, your word ought to be as good as your oath. When you promise something, you do it."

Whatever things ye desire, when ye pray, believe that ye receive them, and ye shall have them.

Mark 11:24

2 The Little Red Wagon

As a child, I often felt my father was unreasonable. I was very sickly, but he seemed determined to teach me to have faith in God for myself. I remember saying one day, "Dad, why do I have to be sick so much? So you can learn to trust God?"

He answered, "It isn't a matter of *my* learning, but God wants *you* to see that believing Him brings results."

One day I went to him with a very special request. I wanted a wagon. We lived on a hill which was over a mile long. We always thought the thrill of the long ride down was worth the weary walk up.

But I didn't have a wagon like the other boys. I pleaded, "Dad, why can't I have a wagon like all the rest of the boys?"

"How do you think I would get a wagon for you?" he said.

"Well," I replied, "I suppose you would pray for it."

"That's right, Richard. God will hear your prayer

as well as mine. Go pray for it."

So off to the bedroom I went and knelt beside my bed and asked God earnestly for a wagon. I was careful to describe exactly the kind I wanted. You can be sure it was to be better and faster than any wagon on the hill!

In the congregation of which my father was pastor at that time, there was a man who owned a general store and who apparently had more money than anyone else in the church. He also gave more money to our church than anyone else, and since my father lived on a "free will offering basis" (i.e., the loose offerings that came in on the collection plates), this man's giving was very important.

But somehow my father had offended the man, and he had quit giving in the loose offerings. By withholding his money he hoped to "starve the preacher out," as they termed it in those days.

My father, however, knew how to trust God. God was his employer and to God he always looked for support. And the wonder to me, as a boy, was that God always raised up and sent in other funds whenever such situations occurred. In fact, as I remember, our family always lived more comfortably when someone was trying to starve us out. God would lay our need upon the hearts of others and what they gave would always more than make up for what some withheld. It was a sublime lesson to me to see how my father would commit such things to his Heavenly Father.

At the age of six, however, I didn't understand all of this. I knew I wanted a wagon. And I also knew that the owner of the general store seemed surprised that my father always paid cash for the previous week's groceries on Monday mornings, as was his custom.

One Monday morning, just as my quarantine period for chicken pox was ending, and for that reason I was at home, my father asked if I would like to go to the store with him. I was delighted to get out of the house. At the store the proprietor was waiting for my father and as my father read him our new grocery list, the storekeeper turned, pointed his finger at me, and in a rough voice which really frightened me said, "Do you want a wagon?"

I stammered, "Y-yes, sir."

"Go to the back of the store and get any wagon you want!" he commanded.

Later on, I learned that the man had not really wanted to give me the wagon, but during many sleepless nights, God had kept him awake, telling him to give the preacher's son a wagon. And that, you can be sure, was fine with me!

> *If the Spirit that raised up Jesus from the dead dwell in you, He that raised up Christ from the dead shall also quicken your mortal bodies, by His Spirit that dwelleth in you.*
>
> Romans 8:11

3 Healing at Our House

When my father and mother were in their late 20s, my mother became seriously ill. After a consultation, the physicians in the small Ohio city in which my parents lived declared her incurable. They went so far as to offer to send her to any part of the world where my father felt he could obtain help for her cure. At the time he owed a year's salary to the physicians and another year's salary to the drugstores. It looked hopeless.

The day arrived when my father was notified that my mother had only three weeks to live. At that time, my father believed that it was heresy to think that God might heal today. Like many others, he believed that the days of miracles were past. In fact, when one of my mother's friends gave her a religious periodical (*The Alliance Weekly*) which contained an account of healing, my father said that my mother should return the magazine, as he didn't want that kind of trash in his house.

The day following the doctor's announcement, however, one of the men who worked under my father at the factory said to Dad as he passed by, "Mr. Harvey, I have an aunt who had internal and external cancer and whom the doctor pronounced incurable. She was prayed for last week by an evangelist holding tent meetings on the outskirts of the city and God healed her. Why don't you take your wife there?"

All day long the words of this man ran through my father's mind. At family worship around my mother's bed that evening my parents, in their systematic reading of the scriptures, read Romans chapter eight, verse 11: "But if the Spirit of him that raised up Jesus from the dead dwell in you, he that raised up Christ from the dead shall also quicken your mortal bodies by his Spirit that dwelleth in you." After reading that my father said, "I always thought this verse referred to our spirits or souls, but it says *mortal* bodies."

In his prayer to God that evening he said, "I have always been taught that You do not heal today. Please show us clearly." All evening and the next day, Romans 8:11 kept going through his mind: ". . . if the Spirit that raised up Jesus from the dead dwell in you, he that raised up Christ from the dead shall also quicken your mortal bodies by his Spirit that dwelleth in you."

By the close of the day his mind was made up. He stopped at the livery stable on his way home from work and engaged a horse and buggy to come and pick up my mother and take her to the house where the evangelist was staying. When he returned home from work that night, he told my mother what he had done. "I won't go," she stated. "Do you think I would go to a stranger's house and have to be waited on, or even soil the bed?"

Father tried to reason with her, but she was adamant. So not being able to persuade her, he decided to say what he felt was cruel, but necessary: "Emma," he said, "you know what the doctors have said. You have a maximum of three weeks to live. If you want me to walk away from the cemetery with three little motherless children, you must assume responsibility."

Sobbing, she replied, "All right, I'll go."

The next morning the livery stable man came to get her to take her to the home where the evangelist was staying. After work my father went after her. He was very excited.

"Are you healed?" he said.

"I'm not sure."

"Are you feeling any better?"

"A little."

"What did the preacher do?"

"Well," she said, "the evangelist took the Bible and read some Scriptures which contained some promises of God to heal. He asked if I believed the Bible. I said, 'Yes.' He had a little bottle of oil and anointed my head with the oil and prayed."

"Is that all?" asked my father.

"Yes, that's all," she said with finality.

My mother improved just enough to encourage their faith. About a week later as my father sat by her bedside reading aloud, my mother interrupted, "Henry, I'm hemorrhaging again!"

On his previous visit, the doctor had given my father a pint of medicine and told him that if my mother started to hemorrhage, he was to give her the whole bottle and come for him as fast as possible. Now they both looked at the medicine and mother said, "What's the use of taking it? Any help I would get would only be temporary. I'll die just the same. We might as well trust God wholly!"

My father fell down at the foot of the bed and buried his head in the bedclothes and prayed. I've heard him say many times as he later related this incident, "I sobbed more than I prayed, because I really didn't know how to pray."

When he lifted his head from the bed my mother's eyes were closed. She lay deathly still. He thought she had died. He felt her pulse, but it was so weak he wasn't sure she had one. Her hand felt cold; he was frightened. He grabbed for a mirror and put it to her mouth to see if she was still breathing. He thought he saw moisture on the mirror. Then he simply sat down by the side of the bed and held her hand.

Dad said he never knew how long he sat there, but that it seemed like hours.

Finally, Mother opened her eyes and said, "Henry, would you please cook me some chicken the way I like it?" That really frightened him. "This must be the last request that the dying often have!" he thought.

But my mother ate well, and for the first time in

many months she went peacefully to sleep. She was still sleeping the next day when it was time for my father to go to work. He was reluctant to leave her, but his debts compelled him. When he came home that evening, my mother met him at the door. She had prepared his evening meal! The next Sunday she walked one and a half miles to Sunday School and home again. Twelve years later she gave birth to me. She lived to be 81 years old.

As a result of this great miracle in my mother's life, my father's strong sense of loyalty brought him to the conclusion that since Christ had healed my mother when no one else could, it was only proper for him to make Christ his only physician and to go to Him for *all* his physical needs. I've heard my father say, "If a physician did for you what no one else could do, would you pass by his office and go to another for your bodily needs?"

Thus, from that time on in my parents' home, we prayed for all the physical needs of our family. Only once after Mother's healing did a doctor ever visit our home, and that was when I was 14 years old. The doctor had run into me with his car and had to bring me home! I'm sure that doctor never forgot the occasion. He and another man carried me upstairs to our second-floor flat and laid me on the couch. My left foot was broken and almost turned around. My father remarked firmly, "The first thing we will do is pray." With that he dropped to his knees.

As soon as he began to pray, my foot snapped back into place. My father signed a statement for the doctor saying that he himself would be wholly responsible for my leg, but granted the doctor's request that he be permitted to take a small X-ray. The X-ray, to everyone's amazement, revealed that God's bonesetting had been perfect. In fact, from that time on, my left leg has been straighter than my right one!

Our family consisted of three boys and one girl. My oldest brother, Lynn, as a young man entered the service of the Lord under the tutelage of a famous evangelist, Paul Rader. Lynn became his private secretary and pianist. But the financial sacrifices of the evangelistic life became too great for him and his family, so he chose what he thought was an easier path and entered the world of business. In the eyes of the world, he became a successful man, reaching a point where he was appointed vice-president in charge of sales at a rubber company.

But many years later, as we three boys stood at the casket of our father, Lynn turned to my brother Earl (also a minister) and me and said, "I guess I missed it. After all, you fellows have everything—a happy home, good health and the satisfaction of helping others in your ministry. My health is broken, my family gone, and my money is about gone too."

My brother Earl became a missionary, first to the Philippines, and then for 15 years to mainland China under The Christian and Missionary Alliance. He then felt an obligation to stay home and educate his four boys. So he entered a seminary for further training and then assumed a Presbyterian pastorate on the West Coast.

My sister Mildred, who was like a queen in our family and a little mother to me, was 13 years older than I. She spent much time teaching me many of life's values. In fact, if I had been asked as a boy whom I loved most in all the world, I would have answered without hesitation, "My sister." She was a graduate nurse and went to the mission field in central China, also under The Christian and Missionary Alliance. After serving only one year, she contracted black smallpox, died and was buried in Hankow, China, in 1919.

Her death was a terrific blow, especially to my mother. And for me as a teenager, it created additional bitterness, although I would never say so openly. Inside me, however, I struggled with a perplexing question: Why, when my sister was so needed and such an effective soul winner, did God take *her*? I really wondered about that. Later, however, I learned of circumstances and events that made me realize that God truly does do all things well.

*I shall not die, but live, and declare the works of the
Lord.*

Psalm 118:17

4 Cross-eyed and Tongue-tied

One July 5, 1905, in a tumbledown shack that
was called a parsonage, in Grove City, Pennsylvania,
a cross-eyed, tongue-tied "blue" baby boy was born
to Emma and Henry Harvey. The parents were told
that it was only a matter of hours before the baby
would die.

Not convinced, the father went immediately to
God in prayer and said, "Even though the
physicians said it was impossible for us to have
another child, You have given us one. Would You
reveal to us what You have to say concerning our
son?" Then, for an answer, he went, as usual, to
God's Word.

In Psalm 118, verse 17, God gave him this
promise: "I shall not die, but live, and declare the
works of the Lord." As far as that young father was
concerned, it was a definite promise to him that the
child would live and serve the Lord. And my father
was right—because over 70 years later, here I am!
But in my early years, my father had to lean heavily
on that promise. It was a tremendous struggle just

for me to live.

When I was 11 months old, I contracted double pneumonia and whooping cough. A nurse who was visiting in the home and assisting my mother came and told my father that I had died. Father said, "Don't tell his mother. He's not dead." He knelt by my crib and reminded God of His promise until he was satisfied that God had answered prayer and the crisis was past.

When I was about a year old, my parents were sure that I was cross-eyed. It was not just a weakness, but something that looked permanent. So one day they clasped their hands over my crib and laid their hands on me and asked God to straighten my eyes. And He did it! (I'm homely enough now, but I'm sure I must have been far worse as a cross-eyed baby!)

Before I was three years old I had contracted black diphtheria, and again someone came and told my father that I had died. Father said, "Well, don't say anything to anybody." He went into the room, shut the door, knelt down by my bed, took hold of my hand, and there he stayed until I moved. He got up, thanked God and went and told my mother that I was all right.

Before I was four years old, a nurse visited our home. My parents said to her, "Our son seems to have normal intelligence." (Now, you may doubt that and think it parental prejudice, but that's what they said.) "But Richard won't talk. We can't get him to say anything." I hadn't even said, "Mama," or "Daddy." Instead I had sounds for everything I wanted.

The nurse looked into my mouth and said, "Reverend Harvey, your son is very badly tongue-tied. There is a string at the roof of his mouth, as well as under his tongue." When she left, my mother and father knelt beside me, laid their hands on me and prayed. Again my father quoted the promise, "I shall not die, but live, and declare the works of the Lord." He prayed, "Lord, you said not only that my son would live and not die, but that he would declare the works of the Lord. He cannot declare your works with his tongue tied."

God loosed my tongue. Sometimes I think He did too good a job—for it has many times gotten me into trouble! I began to speak at four years and some of my relatives said I made up for it in the next two years. One of my uncles called me a windjammer!

At the age of six I was sent to school. I was there one week when I came down with measles and was sent home. At the end of the quarantine period I went back to school. I was in school three more days before I contracted the chicken pox. So I was kept home again for a stretch and after the quarantine period for that, I went back to school. Then it was scarlatina. Again I was kept home. My parents decided to wait until after the Christmas vacation to send me back. I returned but contracted typhoid fever. At the end of that stretch my parents decided I was too weak to go back to school. So in reality I didn't start school until I was seven!

About a year later I began to be conscious of the

fact that I was a sinner. I was on my way out of school one day. It had snowed heavily that morning and the boys had made a slide in front of the school. I tried it, but my feet went out from under me. My head hit the sidewalk and out from my lips came an oath. I couldn't help but say to myself, "Isn't that strange? My father and mother don't swear. That must have come from the inside."

When my father asked me to say grace at the table, I knew God didn't hear me. When I prayed at family worship, I knew God didn't hear me. When I prayed at night before I went to bed, God was silent because there was sin in my heart and it was unconfessed. From the moment that oath slipped out, I was afraid I'd have an accident and die.

One day at a summer camp, sitting in the back of the tent, really not too interested in the meeting, I again became conscious of the guilt on my heart. When the preacher's invitation was given, I waited until the very last line of the last verse of the hymn. Then I walked down the sawdust aisle. I knelt at the altar, confessed my sins and gave my heart and life to Jesus Christ.

Only a person who has experienced this understands the great peace that comes. One seems lighter. Even nature takes on a new look. To some it seems that a heavy burden rolls away. Sin is gone and many fears disappear.

Soon after I took that step, our missionary conference began. With my newfound joy I had a great desire that all the boys and girls around the world would come to know Jesus Christ also. At the dinner table I asked my father if I could make a missionary pledge (a promise to give a specific amount of money within a specific period of time). His reply was characteristic: "Well, son, you can make a pledge if you pay it yourself, but don't expect me to help."

So I began to figure how much money I'd receive in a year's time from running errands and from gifts for special days. My total came to $8.50. After weighing the sacrifice of certain pleasures, I pledged $8.00, reserving 50¢ for refreshments at summer camp.

Soon after the missionary conference came Easter. At Easter, it was my parents' custom to give me 50¢ to purchase Easter candies for my basket. But I had figured that 50¢ into the amount I would receive. Therefore, I knew I had to put it into the missionary bank. It was not easy to do and though I did it, it was not done joyfully.

My father thought he might buy me one candy Easter egg, but decided against it, believing the sacrifice and discipline would do me good. I told my father some years later I was glad God was more merciful than he was, because God laid "my need" on the hearts of two French girls who worked for a wealthy family. Those girls competed to see which one could give me the most Easter gifts! They both brought me a cardboard box full of Easter goodies—the kind of boxes used to bring groceries home from the supermarket. If I took all the other Easter gifts received in my entire life, they would not compare with what those two girls gave me that night before Easter!

But that was not all. That same year God led a drugstore man to give me a bag of candy and chewing gum almost every day on my way home from school. Once in a while he would call me in to the soda fountain and tell me I could choose anything I wanted. Since a banana split was the finest and most expensive item on the glass behind his counter, a banana split was my request.

Thus, early in life I learned that one cannot outgive God. "Give and it shall be given unto you, good measure, pressed down, and shaken together and running over. . . ." That, I have found, is God's response to any sacrifice we ever make.

The pledge, of course, was paid on time!

5 A Dollar and Seventy-seven Cents

Soon after that memorable Easter, my father
expressed his desire to go to Pittsburgh,
Pennsylvania, to be the assistant pastor to the Rev.
E.D. Whiteside, who was noted for his great faith
and unusual answers to prayer. After corresponding
with Rev. Whiteside and receiving an invitation to
come, my father resigned his pastorate in Utica,
New York.

But there were problems in accepting such an
invitation. Mr. Whiteside gave no salary to his
assistants, not even a place to live. Neither was there
an offering ever taken for the assistants at a regular
church meeting. To accept such a job certainly
meant that one had to live completely by faith. So
my father thought it would be wise for my mother
and me to stay at first with my brother Lynn in
Chicago. He needed to study the situation in
Pittsburgh to see what housing arrangements could
be made before having us there.

During our time in Chicago, *The Tribune* ran a

full-page ad about a boat excursion on Lake Michigan. I looked at that ad with great longing. Both my brother and my mother watched me as I stared at it.

"Dick, you'd like to go on that boat, wouldn't you?" Lynn asked.

"I sure would," I replied.

"I'll tell you what I'll do," he said. "We'll put a bank on the table and all of us will put our spare cash into it. The night before the boat sails, we will open the bank. If there is enough for all of us to go, we'll go and if there isn't enough for all of us, then none of us will go. Is this a fair agreement?"

I agreed it was. I was willing to grasp at any hope at all.

We lived in an apartment house on Halstead Street. I ran errands for a doctor, an undertaker and a dentist, who also lived in our apartment. We all did our part in putting what we could into the bank on the table.

As a boy, it was difficult for me to wait for the opening of the bank. The occasion is still fresh in my memory: I can see my brother trying to use a knife to slip the coins out of the acorn crockery bank and because of the slowness of the process, finally taking a hammer and smashing it, causing the money to roll on the table. I was very excited as I watched him count it. And I was heartbroken when he announced it was $1.77 short.

It was more than I could take. I ran out of the house and went behind an old barn that was still at the back of the property and there I burst into tears.

When I got control of myself, I returned to the house and my brother said, "Dick, I think we'd better stick to our agreement. We can't go on the excursion, but tomorrow you and I will go down and watch the big boat sail."

The next morning Lynn and I got up early. After he had done some chores, we took a streetcar to the Chicago Loop. We stood on the bridge at a good vantage point to observe all the excitement on the pier below. The flags were flying, the band was on the ship's top deck playing, and many, many people were waiting to board the ship.

The gangplank was lowered and the chain let down. The people poured onto the boat. In a short time the bell sounded, the whistle blew, and the chain was pulled across the gangplank.

Many of those left behind were very disappointed. Such cursing and swearing I had never heard before! As I remember, one man was permitted to crawl under the chain and go up the gangplank. The bell on the ship rang again, the whistle blew, the gangplank was pulled aboard, and the ropes to the pier were loosened.

And then, before our eyes, that giant ship, the *Eastland*, tipped over in the Chicago River. Something had happened on shore that had caused the ship's passengers to rush to one side. About the only ones saved were those who had been on the top deck. Many of these crawled to shore over the bodies of those beneath them.

Soon, men were piling human bodies on the pier like one might stack boxes. The city sent dump wagons pulled by horses to carry the corpses to the funeral parlors.

God's act of withholding $1.77 had almost certainly saved my life!

> *Train up a child in the way he should go and when he is old, he will not depart from it.*
>
> Proverbs 22:6

6 Pittsburgh Prayers

My years in Pittsburgh were most memorable. It was there I felt the call of God to give Him my life for Christian service. At the time Paul Rader was pastor of Moody Church in Chicago, but he frequently returned to the great missionary conventions held in Carnegie Hall, Pittsburgh.

It was in the Rev. Whiteside's "faith home" in Pittsburgh that I lived with my parents for the first three months. No meals were served on Thursdays in that home—it was a weekly day of fasting and prayer. As a boy I saw many people come on stretchers and in wheelchairs who later walked out whole in answer to the prayers and faith manifested there.

"Faith home," however, could be only temporary quarters. My father kept looking for a place for the four of us (my sister Mildred, my parents and me). I soon discovered that if I were ever to have anything I needed or wanted, I would have to earn it myself. So I started a junk business—old rags, magazines, newspapers, iron, etc. I also sold the *Saturday*

Evening Post, Country Gentlemen, and *Liberty*. As I look back, I am surprised that Mr. Whiteside let me use any space at all to store my junk in his already overcrowded apartments. But I found some space for the stuff under the rear porch. In a month's time, I was earning more money than my father, which in dollars and cents was not saying very much. But the proceeds did give me spending money for school supplies, my own clothes and other needs.

My father finally found two furnished rooms on the third floor of a rooming house, near the corner of Ohio and Western Avenues. That place with all its hardships will live in my memory forever. To approach the rooms we had to climb steep, rickety stairs without the aid of lights, as the landlady was too frugal to let the overhead gaslight burn. Then we had to blindly feel and hunt for the keyhole and try to avoid stumbling through the door!

There were other inhabitants in the apartment besides our family. We hunted for them at night by flashlight. (Oh, if we had only had modern insecticides!) What we had, we sprayed on the bugs and they just crawled out from under it. I still remember the awful odor in the house because of our efforts.

I especially remember one night when I was having great difficulty sleeping. My parents finally got up, lit the gas lamp and made me get out of bed. I had 17 bed bugs for company! (Speaking of the bed, it should have been in a museum. I've never seen another like it anywhere. It was a folding bed that was kept in a box. Sometimes it would decide to fold up of its own accord, and frequently did so. Many nights I awoke with a start to find the mattress jammed against my face and my cries stifled by bedclothes!)

Of course, we always said grace at the table. What I remember most were the many times (I would hesitate to guess how many, because to me, a child, the number probably seemed far greater than it actually was) we sat down to the table and there was no food to eat. The table would be set, we would sit down and my father would say, "Let us pray the Lord's Prayer."

I doubt that you have ever heard a boy pray that prayer as earnestly as I prayed it, especially when we came to the part, "Give us this day our daily bread." I'm sure heaven felt my emphasis, because not once nor twice, not 10 nor 20 times, but always, either while praying or soon after, there would be a knock at the door. Sometimes someone would be there with a prepared meal; at other times food would be left on the door step, often already cooked; and sometimes there would be a box of groceries. I'm sure I would remember if I ever had to go without a meal, but that never happened.

Once I remember my father saying to me, "Richard, I have to go to a neighboring town to pray for a woman who is critically ill. Would you like to ride along on the streetcar? We will have to change cars a couple of times."

"Okay," I said.

We waited on the corner just half a block from our home for a streetcar. When it arrived, my father put me on first. Then, before he could step up, a stranger pushed in ahead of him, dropped three fares in the box and said to Dad, "I just dropped your fare and your kid's also." Afterwards, my father told me he had not had a single penny.

My reaction to that incident was not gratitude to God for His great provision. Instead I was angry in my heart because we had nothing. Each circumstance made me more determined—"I'll never be a preacher and have to live like this."

One of the crises of my life took place in those "upper rooms." One morning at the breakfast table, I became angry over something and pushed some food on the floor. My father got the broom, handed it to me and said, "Son, clean it up."

I threw the broom on the floor.

"Pick it up," he demanded.

"I won't," I replied.

That started about 8:15 a.m. and I was supposed to leave for school at 8:30. The hassle continued through the morning, through the lunch hour (but without lunch and no school), through the day.

"Pick it up."

"I won't."

"Pick it up."

"I won't."

Supper time came, the struggle of wills still going on. About 8:00 p.m. he said, "You will pick up that broom and clean up that mess or there will be no sleep and nothing to eat even if it takes all night or all week." Knowing he was like the rock of Gibraltar and always kept his word, finally, about 9:00 that evening I picked up the broom, cleaned up the mess and washed the floor. Then my father gave me the licking of my life!

The next day he said to me, "Richard, if I had not conquered your will, you would have been useless to God or anybody else, including yourself. That is the last licking I am ever going to give you. I see you want to make your own decisions."

From then on I did.

He would say, "Here is the decision you need to make. If you choose the wrong one, this will be the consequence you will have to pay." I did not like that either.

God spoke to me frequently at family worship, as our family read the Bible together, but I would try not to let my parents know I had been impressed. And when we sang, *To the Regions Beyond I Must Go*, I would often sing, "To the regions beyond I'm supposed to go!"

Yet I was as active in the church as a boy of 10 could be. I remember "Old Daddy Whitesides," as he was affectionately called, saying to me one Sunday morning as I was leaving, "Richard, would you do something for me?"

I answered, "Certainly, Reverend Whiteside."

In his quiet manner of speaking, he said, "People are thoughtless. They leave the songbooks on the pews and then the books drop onto the floor. Would you be willing, after each service, to go through all the rows and put the songbooks in the racks?"

"Yes, sir," I replied. And I sensed within a growing

pride that I could be trusted. After some months he had the chief usher ask me to take up the offering in one of the balcony sections. Within six months he had me downstairs acting as an usher and showed his confidence in me by having me do the same thing at the great annual missionary convention in Carnegie Hall. That did something special to me and for me. I felt I could not let such a man of God down, in spite of my inward fightings.

After about two and one-half years of ministry in Pittsburgh, my father accepted the call to be the pastor of the Alliance church in Erie, Pennsylvania.

Rebellion is as the sin of witchcraft and stubbornness is as iniquity and idolatry.

1 Samuel 15:23

7 The Easter Suit

When you are a teenager, everybody is trying to mold you—parents, school, church, friends and foes. No wonder so many teenagers rebel!

I was no exception. I felt it, I had it—the rebellion that causes so much turmoil in a young person's heart. But my great love and respect for my parents and the faith that had developed in my heart after my conversion kept me from kicking over the traces.

Many times I would have liked to have blown things "sky high" and "painted the town red." As a teenager my rebellion against being a preacher's son was full-blown and some of the experiences I am about to relate only crystallized my determination never to be a minister of the gospel.

My early teen years in Erie, Pennsylvania, were not dull. Though my father's church was small, after his first few months there were several young people with whom I could associate. Plenty of activity both at the church and at school plus a part-time job left little spare time.

During our first days in Erie we lived in a single room at the back of the small church. I remember its furnishings: a bed, three chairs, a stand which we used for a table and a gas stove. Thirty-eight days we lived there and our diet was simple: soft-boiled eggs with bread and butter for breakfast, hard-boiled eggs for lunch and medium-boiled eggs for the evening meal. Once in a while we had jam òn our bread. I became sick eating eggs and developed a distaste for them that lasted until I was about 50 years old.

Oh yes, and the bed—it sank in the middle and the first night that was where I slept—in the middle, between my father and mother. But they both kept rolling my way, so the next night they tried putting me on one side.

I rolled out.

The following night, they put me on the other side.

I rolled out again.

Finally, since all our furniture was in storage and there was no other place for me to sleep, they decided to tie me to the bedposts. My hands were tied to the top posts and my feet to the bottom posts, and I had to notify my parents when I wanted to turn over.

Finally, we moved from the back room of the church when my father located a suitable place. Our new home was a second-floor flat in a fairly good residential section with a school only one block away. It was a nice enough part of the city and the children were generally well clothed. But I had to wear patched trousers and I remember feeling sorry for myself.

One night as my father and I came home from prayer meeting I asked, "Dad, is there any chance of my having a new suit by Easter? Am I going to have to wear patched clothes to church on Easter?" (Although I had been working, I had been getting paid only $1.75 a week. After buying clothes, school supplies and a bicycle for work, I had saved nothing.)

"No, son," he replied, "you won't have to wear patched clothes on Easter. I will get you a suit."

When Good Friday arrived and there was still no suit, I became anxious and asked both my father and mother about the promise. Mother said simply, "If Dad has promised, he'll keep his promise."

Saturday arrived. At the breakfast table I inquired as to when we would go downtown to purchase the suit. "Oh, we'll go," my father reassured me. So I didn't go out to the lot to play as was my custom.

About 10:30 in the morning, I asked again when we would go and got the same answer. At noon I asked again and my dad replied, "Later." Getting more anxious as each hour passed, about mid-afternoon I began to inquire every half hour at my father's study. Each time he would say, "Yes, we will get the suit."

The stores in Erie closed one hour earlier on Saturday, at 5:30, and it took 20 minutes to walk downtown from where we lived. At 5:00 p.m. I became desperate—"Dad, the stores will close in a half hour. Let's go!"

But still he tarried.

At 5:10 the doorbell rang. I took the first landing in one jump, the remaining stairs with the assistance of the side railing. I threw open the door. I looked in both directions, but saw no one. I couldn't figure it out.

My father was right behind me. He stooped down and picked up an envelope that was lying on the threshold. "Come on, Richard, let's go." We ran and we walked and we arrived just as the clerk was preparing to lock the door.

I got the suit for Easter.

And I have often said, "I am going to ask the Lord someday—why, with me, He has always waited until the very last minute to come to my rescue!"

Confess your faults one to another, and pray one for another, that ye may be healed.

James 5:16

8 Conference Encounters

Since I had purposed in my heart to own a big department store, I got a job at Erie's largest. My first job was in the stockroom, then I moved on to the delivery-and-package department. While in that department, I was chosen to deliver very special packages that were not to be trusted to ordinary truck delivery.

At that time they were enlarging the store and space around the outside was filled with building materials. On one particular day those of us who had ridden to work on bicycles had put them on top of a lumber pile. In order to perform a store delivery, I tried to get my bicycle down from the pile, only to have all the bicycles fall on top of me.

I was taken home, more seriously hurt than anyone thought. Five abscesses formed and I hovered between life and death. Two other boys, hurt in similar circumstances, had died. The pain was almost unbearable and I screamed by the hour.

The neighbors pressed my father to take me to the hospital and finally threatened to call the police,

49

who would force him to take me. But my father had promised, in life or death, to trust God alone. He said it was the most trying test of faith he had ever experienced. The devil kept whispering in his ear, "If you loved your son, you would not let him suffer like that." Finally after two days and nights of almost constant praying and fasting, the abscesses broke and there were no aftereffects.

At the age of 18 I attended a summer Bible-and-missionary conference at Beulah Beach, on the shores of Lake Erie, near Vermilion, Ohio. Walking down one of the paths at the conference grounds, I met the evangelist of the conference, Mrs. Cora Rudy Turnbull, who had led me to Christ as a boy of eight.

"This is a happy occasion," said the evangelist, and after a few pleasant remarks, inquired, "By the way, Richard, have you ever given your entire life to Jesus Christ?"

Straightening up and looking the lady in the eye, I said, "If you mean by that, am I willing to be a preacher or a missionary, absolutely not!"

"Well, why not?" she asked.

I retorted, "I would like to be able to eat what I want to eat when I want to eat it, and I would like to be able to wear what I want to wear when I want to wear it."

"Haven't you always had food and clothing?" she asked.

"Yes, if you mean nothing but eggs for 38 days, and if you mean leftover clothing made from dead men's clothes. Here I am 17 years old and I have had but one new store-bought suit in my life. No, it is not for me."

"Richard, I am going to pray for you every day this coming year."

"Go ahead if you think it will do any good," I said and walked away.

As unusual as it may seem, I met the same evangelist at almost the same spot next summer. "Well, imagine meeting you here again, Richard. Do you remember our conversation last year?"

"Yes, I do."

"Well, how do you feel about it now?"

Without hesitation and with a forced smile I said, "Oh, just like I did last year!"

The evangelist seemed a bit startled. "Richard," she said, "I didn't fully keep my promise to pray for you *every* day, though I did pray for you many times. I guess I'll have to pray every day this year."

I answered, "It will do about as much good as it did last year." And again I walked away.

That fall I left for college and during the spring term became very sick. The pastors and elders prayed for me, but I got worse. Finally, the pastor, the Rev. P.R. Hyde, with whom I was rooming at the parsonage, phoned my father and asked him to come for me. At home my temperature kept rising to the danger point and my parents became desperate.

My father asked the elders of the church to come and pray for me and to stay all night if necessary. They came and prayed and about midnight the senior elder came into the room (I had just come out of a delirious state caused by a high fever). He came to my bedside and quietly said, "Richard, when I pray for you, my prayers bounce back from the ceiling. God isn't hearing us. There must be something between you and your God. Thus, it is useless for us to remain here. When you settle whatever is between you and God, you'll be all right."

He picked up his hat and departed with the rest of the elders.

I knew what stood between God and me, but I stubbornly continued to resist. At the break of day, when I felt in my heart that it was life or death for me, I yielded. "Oh God, if You will forgive my stubborn heart and my insistence upon having my own way and will, please heal me. I will preach or do anything that You ask me to do."

Almost immediately the fever subsided. I broke out with such intense perspiration that I soaked a couple of flannel blankets. I was healed.

The very next day I returned to college. It was fortunate that I had only one class that day, because I was still very weak. But as my strength returned, I began to prepare for God's service.

The following summer at the same Bible conference along Lake Erie, I met the girl I was to marry.

Study to show yourself approved unto God, a workman that needeth not to be ashamed. . . .

2 Timothy 2:15

9 College Companions

During my senior year of high school my father said, "If you really want to go to college, I will assist you to the limit of my ability." That limit I knew was very small, but I figured any assistance would be a help.

I sent for the catalogs of several colleges that I knew about, read and studied them and came to my decision. I took from my savings and sent the registration fee to the college of my choice.

That summer at Beulah Beach conference, my boyhood hero, Paul Rader, was one of the speakers. One day I got up enough courage to go to his room at the conference hotel. I knocked at the door and was invited in.

Rader knew me, as he was a personal friend of my father and my brother Lynn had been his personal secretary and traveling pianist. "What brings you here?" he asked.

"This year I go to college, and since you know about the one I have chosen I thought you could give me some information."

When I told him my choice, he said, "Oh, don't go to that school."

"Why not?"

"I think you need a broader education than you would receive there."

Then I asked, "Where should I go?"

His answer surprised me—"If I could choose any college in America for you, it would be Princeton. But it is too late to get in now, and also it is too expensive for you and your family."

I looked at him in amazement at that suggestion. He continued, "Is there a school of comparable quality near your home?"

"Yes, there is Allegheny, but. . . ."

"I know what you are thinking," he interrupted.

"What am I thinking?" I asked.

Then he explained, "I went to that type of school and lost my faith for a while."

"Exactly," I replied, surprised that he could read my thoughts so correctly.

"That is true, I did backslide, but Richard, you don't need to. I had received only a spiritual experience of Christ, without intellectual knowledge of why or how. Remember, the Bible says, 'Be ready always to give an answer to every man that asketh you a reason of the hope that is in you. . . .' With your background I am sure you know why you believe what you believe. If you will maintain your private devotions and be active in a Bible-believing local church, as well as return home at fairly frequent intervals, you can withstand the doubts, questions and criticisms about the Bible."

I took Paul Rader's advice, notified the college to which I had applied that I would not be coming and applied for admittance to Allegheny College in Meadville, Pennsylvania.

I entered Allegheny College in the fall of 1923 and lived at the residence of Rev. P.R. Hyde. Soon I discovered that most of my fellow students joined a fraternity. Two students "rushed" me, as they called it then. Since one of the fraternities had been started by Paul Rader at Hamlin University, I joined that one.

Belonging to a fraternity was a good experience for me, because I had lived a very sheltered life. Until college I had never really seen a deck of cards or had personal contact with many of the temptations that confront most teenagers. I soon discovered that I would have to take my stand for Christ and explain why I believed what I believed.

We had many "bull" sessions, as the fellows called them. If I ran across a question I couldn't answer, I'd go to Pastor Hyde and say, "Doc, how do you counter this one?" And he would carefully explain.

Another P.K. (preacher's kid) from a similar background came to the school that year and was invited to join the same fraternity. Naturally, we became friends.

One day there was some unexpected free time and the fellows decided that rather than study, they'd make it a true holiday. So the card tables came out of the closets and fellows gathered around the tables in fours and began to play poker for pennies.

My friend and I had never seen anything like it so

we stood around and watched. We were both invited to play and were even offered a gift of 50 pennies a piece. We both declined, but the pressure built up, and I decided I had better leave. My friend said, "Dick, I'm going to hang around a bit longer and see what happens."

It was not long until some of the fellows were cleaned out and had to quit. "Come on, Tom, we'll teach you." They tantalized him again with 50 pennies to start. This time he yielded.

Tom caught on fast. Soon he became the winner at his table, then went to the next card table and cleaned them all out and finally became the champ of the fraternity house.

His fame spread to other frat houses and soon he was earning all his spending money playing cards. The next semester he paid his tuition playing poker. By the time he finished college he was a professional gambler. After graduation, Tom decided to ride the 20th Century Limited and the Broadway Limited trains that ran between New York and Chicago, playing poker with the successful businessmen who also rode them.

Ten years later I returned to the college for a reunion. Tom also returned for the event. However, he had to bring with him his Seeing Eye dog. I was shocked when I saw him.

He told me about his escapades and sinful life. "Dick, I am not only blind, but the doctors tell me I have only three more years to live. I've returned to the fold of God and the past has been forgiven, but my life is ruined, and it all started that day we had a holiday. You left when the men started to play, but I stayed on and learned to play poker. From then on, it was downhill."

In my second year, the son of a multimillionaire came to the college. His grandfather was the first partner of John D. Rockefeller. That fellow was given $400 a month for spending money and a new car every year. He also wore the symbol of affluence—a coon-skin coat. I was attempting to go through college on $400 a year! (In fact, for several years my financial record was placed in the annual catalog to show what could be done by someone willing to make the sacrifice.)

Eugene and I became fast friends. One semester he persuaded his father to pay for my tuition. I often borrowed books because I could not afford to buy them. Sometimes he would buy me the book if I borrowed it too frequently.

One winter evening the fraternity house seemed empty. I was sitting alone in the lounge gazing blankly into the crackling wood fire when Eugene came in and sat down beside me. We both sat in silence for a while staring into the fire.

Finally he spoke softly, "Dick, what makes you different from all the rest of us? You seem to have something that satisfies you even though you have nothing materially. You seem happier than I am. Already I have been around the world three times. I receive a new car every year. I am engaged and my parents have promised to pay for our honeymoon around the world, if we want that. My grandmother is furnishing our home. Already my fiancee is choosing room by room the furnishings we want and my grandfather has agreed to buy it. My father has deposited $100,000 in the bank in my name to set me up in business when I graduate. But I don't have what you have."

So I explained to Eugene that I had Jesus Christ, the joy and satisfaction of His presence within me and that he could have the Savior too.

There was another rather long silence, and then he spoke, "But Dick, I can't pay the price. If I would take your way, I'd be disinherited. I couldn't take that." He got up sorrowfully and left his seat by the fire, just like the rich young ruler who came to Jesus so long ago.

The end of the story is that in 1933 during the depression, Eugene committed suicide. I never knew why. Perhaps he failed in business and lost everything. The words of Jesus seem so true—"He that would save his life shall lose it. . . ."

> *. . . my God shall supply all your need according to his riches in glory by Christ Jesus.*
>
> Philippians 4:19

10 The View from the Balcony

In spite of the help from Eugene, my second year was very difficult. I finished the year in debt and spent all summer selling aluminum kitchenware from house to house, earning only enough to pay up my back debts.

I did not want to return to college unable to pay my tuition and told my parents so. I was adamant in my decision.

One day, though, my mother cried on my shoulder and begged me to let Father borrow the first semester's tuition from the bank. At first I refused, but then I sat down and wrote out a contract for my mother and father to sign. I would accept the borrowing of the tuition, provided that when the note came due, if none of us had the money on hand to pay the bank note, with interest, they would permit me to quit college and go to work to clear the obligation.

And I added, "And, Mother, you won't cry."

"I'll try," is all she would answer.

On weekends I would come home and ask

Mother, "Does Dad have anything toward that note at the bank?" "Not that I know of," was the usual answer. "Well, you'd know if he had any," I'd say in a skeptical voice.

I spent the week before the note was due scrubbing walls and porches to earn some cash. So instead of hitchhiking, I was able to buy transportation home on the train that ran between Erie and Meadville. I packed up all my clothes and school equipment and checked my trunk and suitcase through to Erie, thoroughly expecting not to return to college, but to start work the next week to pay off the note.

Since my father received only the loose offerings from the Sunday collection plates, it was not difficult to reasonably guess how he was doing financially.

That Sunday it rained, showered sleet, and froze. It was almost impossible to walk and exceedingly dangerous to drive. The streets were sheets of ice. There were only a few people at church and they were mostly young people.

When the offering was taken, I stepped out of my seat and went up to the balcony where I could plainly see the offering plates as they were passed. It was mostly small change, plus a couple of bills. So after we got home, I didn't even ask my father how the offering was—I knew we'd be lucky to eat that week.

That night the weather was not much better and the evening congregation was even smaller. There were just two adults present. But, I thought, one never knows what God will do, so I went to the balcony again to watch the contents of the offering plates. Not so much as one bill was dropped in.

When I arrived home I got out the Sunday paper and went through all the want ads. I cut out every job ad that appealed to me. I pasted them on a card in the order of my preference with the idea that on Monday morning right after breakfast I'd start pounding the pavement in search of work.

Between three and four o'clock Monday morning, my father came into the bedroom and wakened me.

"Get up, I want to show you something."

"I'll see it in the morning, I want to sleep."

"Get up now," he said and threw the bedclothes off.

Angrily and groggily I got out of bed and was led by the arm to the dining room where he handed me a check for $200.00.

"Where did you get this?" I asked.

"Last night as I left the church, Scott (one of my father's elders) put something in my pocket. When I woke up a few minutes ago, I remembered what he had done, so I got up and this is what I found in the envelope."

"Dad, it couldn't be for you. You never have been given that much at one time in your whole life!"

"All right, son, we'll go to his home in the morning before he goes to work and find out what it is for, but you'll have to be up by six."

The next morning, without breakfast, we set out for Scott's place in the country. On the way I made my father promise to follow a certain procedure in his queries. "Dad, ask him if this is for foreign missions. If he says no, then ask him if it is for the building fund. If he still says no, ask him what it is for."

"What brings you people here at this early hour?" Scott asked.

"It's about that check you put in my pocket last night at church."

My father did as he had promised. "No," was the emphatic answer to each question.

"The check is for you personally. It is made out in your name, isn't it?" Then he continued, "Pastor, yesterday in all that storm, a creditor of mine told me, with cursing, that he would never give me a cent of what he owed me for painting his house. I promised God that if He would make that man pay me, I'd give it all to my pastor. In that storm last night he came, almost pushed his way into the house, threw the money on the table and shouted, 'Here, take your money! I can't eat or sleep because of you!' So I was only keeping my promise to God—it's yours."

So that same day I packed up again and returned to college.

To me it is a most remarkable thing that under the same circumstances involving the same man, Scott, God answered the same kind of prayer in March of the next year. In all my years of experience, it is the only occasion in which God answered prayer in the same way twice.

> . . . if two of you shall agree on earth as touching
> any thing that they shall ask, it shall be done for
> them of my Father which is in heaven.
>
> Matthew 18:19

11 The Flask Story

The college experience I am about to tell now has left the most lasting impression upon me of any. I have told it all over the world for more than 40 years. Suddenly it began to appear in print in many magazines, in different languages and under various titles, sometimes under my name, sometimes not.

Probably the most popular class at the college was the first-year chemistry class. It was definitely the largest. Most every student took the class sometime during his four years regardless of his major. But since it was a first-year subject, most took it their freshman year.

Dr. Lee was the most noted and honored professor in the college. He had had many honors bestowed on him from numerous scientific societies around the world. His influence carried more weight than that of any of the other teachers. He insisted that he believed in God as the creator of an original mass that was thrown into space and that God had set a group of laws to govern it. He also believed that

God no longer paid any special attention to the earth as far as man was concerned. He believed it was useless for man to try to get God's attention, much less His intervention.

Among many involved themes in his lectures, Dr. Lee chose the subject of prayer—a series of three lectures given annually the week before Thanksgiving recess. The second lecture emphasized the thought that there was no such thing as a miracle. After that class when some of the students were gathered around him I said, "Dr. Lee, I have proof of a miracle. I know a man named Jerry Sproul whose vocal cords were destroyed by gas in World War I. He was declared incurable by three army hospitals and thus given an irrevocable pension. He is well known by all the officials of the Pittsburgh, Pennsylvania, City Hall and reporters of that city. After he was prayed for, he received new vocal cords. His medical records are obtainable and I will be glad to obtain them for you."

Dr. Lee's answer was, "I don't believe in any such thing. If there is such an unusual circumstance as you describe, it must have some scientific explanation." And he turned aside.

Dr. Lee's third lecture was on the subject of the impossibility of an objective answer to prayer. He said he would prove his contention. At the end of his lecture he announced that he would step down from his platform onto the concrete floor. Then he would challenge, "Is there anybody here who still believes in prayer?" And he would say, "Before you answer, let me tell you what I am going to do and what I am going to ask you to do. I will turn around, take a glass flask and hold it at arm's length." Then he would continue, "If you believe that God answers prayer, I want you to stand and pray that when I drop this flask, it won't break. I want you to know that your prayers and the prayers of your parents and Sunday school teachers, and even the prayers of your own pastor cannot prevent this flask from breaking. If you wish to have them here, we will put this off until you return after the Thanksgiving recess."

No one had ever accepted Dr. Lee's challenge.

But one year a certain freshman learned about Dr. Lee's dare. And decided prayerfully that he would accept the challenge. He believed that God had given him the promise, ". . . if two of you shall agree on earth as touching any thing that they shall ask, it shall be done for them of my Father which is in heaven." Then the young man sought out another Christian to stand with him in prayer for courage and faith and they believed together that God would keep the flask from breaking.

The day came. At the end of the final lecture on prayer, the annual challenge was put forth as it had been for 12 years. As soon as Dr. Lee asked, "Is there anyone here who believes God answers prayer?" the young man stepped into the aisle and raised his hand and said, "Dr. Lee, I do."

"Well, this is most interesting. But young man, you had better let me explain what I am going to do and then we'll see if you still desire to pray. I wouldn't want you to be embarrassed before this class."

The professor then took the glass flask and held it out in front of him over the cement floor. "Now I ask you to pray—if you still want to do it—that this flask won't break. After you pray, I'll drop it and I can assure you that it will hit the cement floor and break into hundreds of pieces, and that no prayer can prevent it. Do you still want to pray?"

"Yes, Dr. Lee, I do."

"Well," said the professor, "this is most interesting." And turning to the class he said sarcastically, "Now we will be most reverent while this young man prays." Then he turned to the young man, "Now you may pray."

The freshman just lifted his countenance toward heaven and prayed, "God, I know that You can hear me. Please honor the name of your Son, Jesus Christ, and honor me, Your servant. Don't let the flask break. Amen."

Dr. Lee stretched his arm out as far as he could, opened his hand and let the flask fall. It fell in an arc, hit the toe of Dr. Lee's shoe, rolled over and did not break. There was no movement of air and there were no open windows. The class whistled, clapped and shouted. And Dr. Lee ceased his annual lectures against prayer.

Just a few years ago at a Bible conference in Ontario, Canada, I related this story briefly. After the service, a woman said to me, "Dr. Harvey, I too was a freshman in Dr. Lee's class and heard him make that challenge. What you say is all true."

. . . woe is unto me if I preach not the gospel!
1 Corinthians 9:16

12 A Nervous Wreck

When I entered college, my father had given me one stipulation for his financial help. "Richard, I want you to have more than one handle to your life's basket. You may be planning now to enter some form of Christian ministry, but how do you or I know what might happen? I want you to be able to teach."

Therefore, he demanded that I obtain a State Teacher's Certificate. And so it was that I had three majors—chemistry, biology and education.

At that point I sought the counsel of the Foreign Secretary of our society. I asked if he had any advice concerning my preparation for the mission field. He encouraged me to change my course and, if possible, to take the premed. He suggested that I become a physician and apply for service in Ecuador among the Auca Indians.

So I went to summer school that year and took all the science courses the college would permit and returned my senior year to take the heaviest schedule of my college years—22 hours.

I received my Teacher's Certificate, which I have never used.

I then applied to the medical school of the University of Buffalo and was accepted.

Because I was interested in the mission field as well as medicine, I began to talk to my father about pastoring a small church while I studied. I did find a church, but it proved to be more than I had bargained for. It had financial problems and many other kinds of problems. Finally I found myself actually trying to live on a milkshake a day. Once in a while I had a sandwich to go with it, and occasionally I had a good Sunday dinner.

With the pressures of the church, problems of finance, studies at medical school and many nights with just two or three hours of sleep, my body began to feel the strain. I became very nervous. I could not sit in a class for more than 20 minutes at a time. I would get up and walk out for a drink of water or just walk a bit and return to class. Near the end of that first year, the times I left the class became more frequent and my minutes in class became fewer. During final exams one of my professors phoned my father and suggested he come and get me before I cracked up.

"What are you here for?" I queried.

"Oh, someone from the school called me and said you were sick, and I had better come and take you home."

Stunned and thoroughly shaken, I returned home with my father. But within me grew a great bitterness toward God and man. "What kind of a

God is it that would let this happen to me when I am preparing for His service?" I would ask myself.

Instead of improving, I began to get worse. One day, my father said, "Richard, I am going to be out of town next Sunday. Would you preach for me?"

"Sure, Dad."

No one at church that day ever forgot that sermon. I preached from the text, "Woe unto you, scribes and Pharisees, hypocrites! For ye are like unto whited sepulchres . . . full of dead men's bones." I told them all I knew about them (and that was plenty because I had lived there over 10 years).

When the service was over the senior elder said as he went out, "Richard, don't you think you were pretty hard on us this morning?"

I straightened up and replied tartly, "Sir, if the shoe fits, wear it."

Five years later that same congregation called me to be its pastor. Extending the call to me was real proof of true Christian forgiveness and grace.

During those days of recuperation I was working for a painting contractor from my father's church. He understood my physical condition and let me work as much or as little as I could—and still paid me the going apprentice wage. He also took all the criticism of the church people that welled up from bitterness in my heart. He would smile and say, "They aren't *that* bad." His goodness and Christian example even made me angry at times.

At one point this Christian gentleman took me to Canada for five days of fishing and all he required was that I buy my own fishing license. Truly, Scott

Grames was God's instrument to keep me from exploding.

One day I didn't go to work. My parents were out calling and I was home alone. As I paced the floor, God began to talk to my heart.

"You profess to be a Christian and you have not been reading or praying." I had to agree to that.

"All right," I thought, "I had better get the Bible and try to read something."

Knowing the Psalms were near the middle and looking for a "safe" passage, I shoved my fingers in at about the right place. The Bible slipped out of my hand and fell to the floor, open to First Corinthians chapter nine, verse sixteen. The passage seemed to stand out in large letters: ". . . woe is unto me, if I preach not the gospel!" That made me angry.

My mother's Bible was lying on a table nearby. So I grabbed it and hastily tried again to open it to the middle. It too fell out of my hands onto the table, open to 1 Corinthians 9:16: ". . . woe is unto me, if I preach not the gospel!" That made me angrier, because I had again withdrawn my commitment to Christ and had determined not to be a preacher.

To myself I said, "My father hasn't been reading in Corinthians." So I went to my father's study, picked up his large study Bible, softly laid it down again and slowly and deliberately opened it. It seemed that an unknown hand just turned the pages and in about three turns that Bible too was open to 1 Corinthians 9! That made me so angry I picked up the Bible, flung it against the wall and ran hurriedly out of the house.

70

I went down to the streetcar line, took the first car that came along and rode to the edge of the city. Then I walked and walked until I came to some woods. When I got to what I thought was the center of the woods, I looked up to the sky and began to scream out to God in my pent-up anger.

Then I broke and the tears began to flow. In earnest I began to plead for forgiveness for my bitterness, pride, hatred and backslidings. Peace came to my heart. The turmoil which had been like a troubled sea inside of me suddenly became calm.

I returned home, went to bed and slept all that night and all the next day and night. When I awoke my parents were sitting anxiously beside my bed. God had put a deep sleep upon me. It was His way to bring restoration to my nervous system and my entire body. In a few days I was as one who had never been a nervous wreck. God had completely healed me.

That week I wrote our district superintendent, asking if he had a church where I could candidate. I also wrote to my fiancee in Ohio.

A new day was dawning for us.

> *Who can find a virtuous woman? For her price is far above rubies. The heart of her husband doth safely trust in her, so that he shall have no need of spoil.*
>
> Proverbs 31:10–11

13 A Whirlwind Romance

A tornado played its part in bringing Dorothy Elizabeth Winder and me together. It all happened in the summer of 1924 at the Bible conference at Beulah Beach, Ohio. Her family's tent was almost side by side with my family's. Both families had arrived a couple of days before the conference sessions actually began.

I made it my business to leave my tent about the same time that Miss Winder left hers. But when I eased into asking for a date, "No . . . that is impossible."

Normally, I would have accepted a "no" from a girl, but not this one. I liked her the moment I saw her. The next time I met her was near the old wooden tabernacle.

"By the way," I said, "I am hoping to drive to Lorain to see the devastation caused by the recent tornado. Wouldn't you like to come along?"

"Yes, I'd like to, but you see I promised my father

before I left home that I wouldn't date at camp this year. He thought I was dating too much in high school this past year and so has laid down some strict rules for me here."

We talked for a while. I told her where I attended college and she explained that she would have to work a year to help defray expenses before she could go to Bible school the next fall.

Just then my father passed us to go into the tabernacle.

"That's my father," I pointed out proudly.

"Is that *your* father? I've wondered who that stately looking gentleman is. With his white hair, mustache and beard, he looks like an English duke to me. I've admired him so much." (She told me afterward that after that my stock with her went up about 100 percent!)

"Why don't you ask your mother if she'll give you permission to go to Lorain with me tomorrow?" I persisted.

Dorothy did ask and received the necessary permission. I was walking on air the rest of the day.

The date was all I could have hoped for. Dorothy was easy to get acquainted with as we happily drove along. She told me she had given her life for service to the Lord. She sat close enough, so I knew she was not afraid of me and did not resent me. It gave me the courage on the way home after inspecting the damage done by the tornado (of course, that had become somewhat of a side issue by that time) to ask her to go with me the next day to see another interesting place called the "Blue Hole." She told me she would have to ask her mother as she thought the permission for the present date was a one-time concession.

Mrs. Winder and I had had some interesting conversations by this time concerning Christ's second coming and many other spiritual matters. Thus she told her daughter that she had no objections to her dating me, but that when her father came at the end of the week it would probably be the end of it.

Against Dorothy's objections, I was waiting with her at the tracks on Friday afternoon when Mr. Winder arrived. She introduced us to each other and then I picked up his suitcases and packages and the three of us started to walk toward the tents.

We talked about the services, the speakers and the wonderful "after services" that were occurring each night in the tabernacle. He was friendly, unexpectedly so. In fact, Dorothy told me later that he had said, "Honey, that's the kind of fellow I wish you'd date." Well, you can be sure, we saw a lot of each other after that.

Every moment I was with her was a thrill. I was falling in love! Her hand sent chills up and down my spine. I remember the night I kissed her goodnight before she went to her tent . . . I couldn't sleep for hours!

On Sunday, the day before we were to part, I asked two favors: Could we write to each other and could I come to see her?

My first trip to Mt. Vernon was the longest 260 miles I had ever traveled. It seemed to take forever.

In those days the roads were just fair and the tires not so good. (Speaking of tires, when I arrived, her local boyfriend kept driving past the house. On my second day there, he placed nails in front of all my tires—and I drove over them!)

I remember saying to Dorothy, "I don't blame Carlos. I think I would be annoyed too at some out-of-town fellow horning in on me and my girl. I have the advantage, staying at your home and being with you all day. Maybe I ought to be a good sport and leave." I hoped, of course, that she wouldn't hear of it.

Her answer surprised me. "If you do that, then I'll never have anything to do with either of you again."

Dorothy and I began writing each other once a month. When I left I was invited back for Thanksgiving. When I arrived, I found that her parents had arranged for me to be invited along with them to have Thanksgiving at Marion, Ohio, with relatives. Before we drove away, they asked if they could put some packages and luggage in the back seat of my car. It was piled high.

As Dorothy and I passed through towns, people turned around to look at us and point, and even laugh. Yes, we were sitting close together. She looked at me and said, "These people think we are honeymooners."

There was a long silence.

"How would you like it if we were on our honeymoon?"

There was a longer silence.

"Let's!" she said, and we both started to laugh,

realizing the significance of it all.

We began to discuss our future. We decided we would think earnestly and pray about our relationship until Christmas and we would cut all entanglements if this was to be an engagement. We would make our final decision during the Christmas vacation.

Between the Thanksgiving visit to Mt. Vernon and the next visit during the Christmas season, we wrote every day. This letter-writing ritual was to keep up for four years, until both of us had a trunk full of letters which we later moved around until our children got into them. Then we burned them as we didn't think they needed that kind of an education!

It was customary in those days on the college campuses to exchange fraternity pins in lieu of an engagement. The pin was a token meaning "engaged to be engaged."

I remember arriving at her home in the middle of the night, the day after Christmas. When I gave her the "uke" which I had specially chosen because of her musical inclinations, she seemed pleased, but the real glow came when I presented her with the fraternity pin. That was really what she was looking for—a pledge of our love.

During the four years of our engagement we managed to see each other four or five times a year. The big event came my last year at college when she came for our formal fraternity banquet. I remember being hardly able to wait to introduce my sweetheart to all my fraternity brothers.

We were married on a bitterly cold, windy day in

1929 in the home of the Winders at Mt. Vernon. We had $75.00 between us and rode back to Erie with my parents. Our honeymoon was spent in the Erie parsonage, the only place we could afford.

Our first week of married life must have been difficult for the new bride. We moved into four cold, dirty rooms over an empty store building which Pastor Hyde had rented for us. Our furniture, except for a daybed which my parents had given us for a wedding present, came out of the cellars and attics of my father's parishioners.

We started evangelistic meetings almost immediately and the new bride had the evangelist to entertain. At the same time, she was trying to clean and settle the rooms at a temperature that was near freezing except by the fireplace, the one cheery spot in the whole place.

In retrospect this may all sound appallingly drear, but in reality there never was a happier bride and groom than Dorothy and Richard Harvey. We were finally able to start our life-work together. We were blissfully content.

There were born to us four children: Daniel Richard, David Paul, Marilyn Ruth and John Arnold.

Two of our sons are foreign missionaries. Daniel serves in Guam with Trans World Radio and David in Guinea, Africa, with The Christian and Missionary Alliance. John is President of the Alliance College of Theology in Australia and Marilyn is married to an Episcopal clergyman in the United States.

If ye shall ask anything in my name, I will do it.
John 14:14

14 The Watermelon Story

We started from scratch to launch a church in Clarion, Pennsylvania. We needed a location and believing that the best one was none too good, I started looking in that part of town most accessible to the people. At that time there was no public transportation and few people had cars.

I found the place—a vacant lot almost in the center of town. I walked around its periphery, praying and claiming the ground for God. Later, the owner's daughter told us we could rent the lot for the fine sum of $5.00 per month.

Then we borrowed $200.00 from my wife's parents and $100.00 from the bank. That was the limit of my borrowing power.

Next, I found a handyman who, with the help of his brother-in-law at 75¢ an hour, was willing to put up our building. We went out to a sawmill in the hills nearby and purchased raw lumber for $30.00 per thousand feet. For the foundation we used concrete blocks. We laid them on the frozen ground, end to end, with no cement.

Then we put two-by-twelves on the blocks and put up raw sheeting for the sides with spaces for windows every six feet. Then we covered the entire structure with roofing paper. We called it our tar paper shanty.

One end we divided into three very small rooms—a living room, a kitchen and a bedroom. The bathroom served both the church and ourselves.

As I look back, it seems rather rugged, but Dorothy and I were radiantly happy. I think our blissfulness, love for each other and enthusiasm were our greatest assets, because I certainly could not preach.

It was a good thing I didn't know how poor a preacher I actually was. My first sermons were from 10–12 minutes in length. And sometimes I hit the climax at eight minutes and had nothing more to say.

When our church was dedicated, the district superintendent, Reverend S.W. McGarvey, made the remark, "There is nothing to worship here but God." How true! You would have believed it if you had seen the auditorium.

In our first year, the attendance averaged about 12 in the morning service, 40 in Sunday school and 60 or more in the evening service if there was something special to attract the townsfolk.

Gradually we grew to 30 in the morning service and over 60 regularly at night. But during the long hot summer, the bottom seemed to drop out and I never did know why.

I wanted to quit. The devil told me I was a failure and that I was in the wrong profession. When I expressed my feelings to my wife, she said, "You can quit if you want to, but I'm staying here. If you think I'm going to live with your parents or go running back to mine, you've got another thought coming. Let's get down to praying more and working harder." So we fasted and prayed and called at least once a month on everybody who had ever come to the church.

That had its advantages. No other pastor in town had time to call on every home once a month and besides that, the town had a wonderful custom.

No matter what the home or who the preacher or priest, if he stopped at a home, whatever the reason, he was always given a gift when he left. Usually it was whatever seemed plentiful. That fall everyone seemed to have a pear tree, so I kept bringing home pears. We did everything that summer that had ever been done with pears—canned them, pickled them, made pear jam, pear butter and even tried to dry them. We had pears under the bed, under the chairs and under the table. That year they came so thick and fast we even went out in the back yard and buried them (at midnight).

By then, Dorothy and I were expecting our first child. One morning after breakfast she said, "I crave something so much that if I don't get it, I don't think I can stand it."

"What do you want that much?"

"A piece of watermelon!"

All I could say was, "Let's pray." So we dropped

on our knees and I cried, "O Lord, send us a watermelon or the money to buy one."

But she said, "We couldn't use the money for a watermelon when we have these utility bills to pay. We had better just believe for a watermelon."

"When do you have to have it?"

"Today."

I raised my hands toward the ceiling and prayed simply, "God, she wants it today."

So I went calling to help God out. I called from about 9:30 a.m. to 5:00 p.m. I don't believe I missed the home of anyone who had ever darkened the door of our little church. I even called on all the business people who had frequently given me something. But nobody, and I mean nobody, gave us a pear or a loaf of bread or anything. The custom surely had failed that day! Even the mailman didn't walk on our side of the street. There wasn't even any junk mail.

It was Thursday, our midweek prayer meeting night. The usual eight people were present. As was our custom after church, Dorothy and I returned to our living quarters and talked over the service. What could we do to make it better? How could we be more helpful to the people who came? And I would ask her what I had done wrong or if she had noticed any mistakes.

When 10:00 came, she spoke up and said, "Well, it's time for bed and no watermelon."

I felt that needed some reply, so I casually answered, "Well, it isn't midnight yet."

Just then a knock came at the door. I opened it

and the man standing there bypassed me, stuck his head in the door and asked my wife, "Could I borrow your husband for a few minutes?" (I think about then she would have loaned him to anybody.)

"Certainly," was her answer.

Then he said to me, "Let's take a walk to town." As we walked, he continued, "Does your wife like ice cream?" It was this traveling salesman's idea that the only place open in our small town at that hour would be a drugstore. He didn't know that the drugstore closed at 9:00.

On our way, we passed an Italian fruit stand. I never knew it to be open evenings, but that night it was.

"Does your wife like oranges?"

"Yes."

He stopped, saw some nice looking oranges, then turned to the shopkeeper, "Give me a half-dozen of those oranges." Then he noticed some bananas. "Does your wife like bananas?" I gave the same affirmative reply. He then picked up a bunch of bananas and gave them to the clerk. I thanked my kind friend and walked out to the sidewalk. On the way out, he spied some watermelon under a table. Through the screen door he called, "Does your wife like watermelon?"

"Yes." That was about all the time I had to reply, for he was already asking the storekeeper: "Would you exchange those oranges and bananas for a watermelon?" He took them from me and thrust into my hands the long-anticipated melon!

I was so excited I don't remember even thanking

him. I ran down the street with the watermelon in my arms, yelling, "I've got it, I've got it, I've got it!"

I jokingly told some of my close friends that someday I was going to ask the Lord why He had not let us keep the oranges and bananas too!

The following summer when I met the traveling salesman again, he explained what had happened. He planned that day just to pass through our town, but when he came to our city limits he felt sick. And when he got to the center of town he was so sick he feared to drive any longer. He pulled up in front of the only hotel, registered and went to bed. It was 5:00 p.m.

Then for five hours, he said, he argued with God, because an inner voice kept saying, "Go over and get Harvey and take him to town."

"No, no. Tomorrow I'll do it."

But the impression got stronger and stronger until he knew that if he were going to get any sleep at all, he would have to obey. He said he did not have the least idea what he was to buy for the young preacher.

I must say that probably nothing in my lifetime has brought to me a clearer revelation of God's personal interest in the details of our lives. He even cared enough to satisfy my wife's intense craving for a piece of watermelon!

> *But the manifestation of the Spirit is given to every man to profit . . . the self-same Spirit dividing to every man severally as he will.*
>
> 1 Corinthians 12:7,11

15 God's Good Gifts

It is my belief that no person is qualified to minister the things of God or deliver the message of the gospel until he has first been filled with the Holy Spirit.

When I was a teenager, I sought on three occasions to be filled with the Holy Spirit. The first two times I went away dissatisfied. The reason, I see now, is largely because I was looking for a feeling and some outward manifestation. God's order, however, is fact, faith, and only then, feeling.

When I was 19, in desperation, I sought again to be filled with the Holy Spirit. A great saint of God said to me, "Richard, you're looking for feeling, but neither the feeling nor the gifts of God will come until you take God's Word at face value. The Bible says that God gives His Holy Spirit to those who ask Him (Luke 11:13) and to those who obey Him (Acts 5:32)."

At 19 I again made a total commitment of my life to God. I reminded God of His promises and

85

accepted them at face value. And I arose to live my daily life claiming the promise that His Spirit lived within and controlled my life.

In a few days I experienced more spiritual reality in my life than I could contain. I had victory over what had been my special weakness—a bad temper. The first proof was my lack of anger when Dorothy's boyfriend Carlos punctured my tires!

A few days later I confronted a spiritualistic medium who had more satanic power than anyone I had ever known. This medium had an international reputation among occultists, but was daily coming to Dorothy's mother, Mrs. Winder, for prayer and deliverance.

One day Dorothy and her parents and I were going to drive to a certain city and this woman wanted to come along. I consented and the five of us started out.

We had been driving about 15 minutes when the spiritualist went into one of her trances. So I thought I'd do what they did in the Scriptures. I said, "In the name of Jesus Christ, come out of her."

They came out all right—but they attacked me. I became paralyzed and had to tell Dorothy, "Grab the wheel! Quick!" I was incapable of controlling the car and very scared.

Mrs. Winder said, "Richard, we'll pray for you." So they prayed and I became perfectly normal. But the spiritualist went into another trance and as far as I was concerned, she could stay in it. I wanted nothing more to do with her.

I'm thankful Mrs. Winder understood. She said,

"Richard, you're up against a battle and you'd better win it. If you don't, you'll be running from the devil all the days of your ministry."

"What do we do?" I said.

Her answer surprised me. "We'll sing!"

"We'll what?!" I managed.

"We'll sing," she repeated. "We'll sing and we'll pray and we'll 'hide you in the name of Jesus' and 'cover you with His blood.' And then you can command the demons safely."

So they began to sing some good gospel songs about the power of the blood of Christ. And after seven songs or so, we pulled over to the side of the road and they prayed as she had suggested.

Then I turned to the spiritualist, who was in the back seat, and simply said, "In the name of Jesus Christ, come out of her."

Before I said those words she had been writhing on the seat and tearing at her clothes. It had taken Dorothy and her parents to hold her down. Now she lay so still I feared she was dead! But after 10 minutes or so, she sat up and was normal.

That day I learned something about the power of the blood of Jesus Christ. And about the power of spiritual song to combat the enemy, the devil.

As a young pastor, I increasingly began to feel the need for divine equipment in my ministry. I had neither preaching ability nor the ability to bring people to the point of deciding for Christ. And I had great difficulty in formulating good original outlines for sermons.

So I began to pray daily that God would give me

some spiritual gifts. And I especially and desperately asked for the gift of teaching. I would pray, "Oh God, make me a great Bible teacher." Within, I was really asking Him to make me a great Bible teacher like someone I knew.

After many weeks of this, while praying one day, it seemed to me a voice from within said, "Are you not willing for me to choose the gift I want to give you?" I was startled.

Out loud, I said, "All right, Lord."

Shortly afterwards, I was ordained to the public ministry at our district conference held in Pittsburgh, Pennsylvania. In the charge to the budding preachers, the speaker said, "Now, when the hands of the elders are laid upon you, expect the Holy Spirit to give to you today a special gift of God for your ministry."

One of the founders of our society, the Reverend William McArthur, prayed when the brethren laid their hands on me. "Oh God, give this young man the gift of evangelism and whatever he needs to accompany this gift."

I returned home on Friday. On Sunday my entire congregation was aware that I was different. Something had happened to my sermons and for the first time people responded to the invitation to seek the Lord. Men and women began to come forward to the altar in my meetings. And from then on, there has always been the evangelistic emphasis in my ministry, even in my Bible teaching and expository preaching. These gifts and others have remained with me and are "without repentance" so far as I am concerned.

My wife and I then applied for service as foreign missionaries. We were examined by some outstanding men of God. Each member of the examining committee seemed to throw up roadblocks. One said the background of Dorothy's parents' health would make her a health risk. Another suggested that if we were accepted, I could go as a teacher in our theological training school in Japan. To this I replied, "That is not my gift, although I am educationally qualified."

One of the brethren said, "I believe God wants this couple to remain in the homeland and send other candidates out, as well as the funds to support them."

It seemed that everything was negative and so was the vote of the committee. My wife was exceedingly disappointed, but I was determined I would do more for God and missions than if we had gone. I believe God helped me to do just that. In all, 108 young people from my pastorates entered full-time service in the Lord's work and more than half of these went to the mission fields of the world.

But this story goes on and on. After more than 40 years in the homeland ministry, my wife and I were appointed by the Foreign Department of the same society, The Christian and Missionary Alliance, for world evangelism for a three-year period. More will be written concerning this later.

*And Jehoshaphat feared, and set himself to seek the
Lord, and proclaimed a fast throughout all Judah.*

2 Chronicles 20:3

16 Fasting for Results

Shortly after my ordination, I was extended a call
to go to Meadville, Pennsylvania, where I had
attended college and lived in the pastor's home. I
was not even required to candidate as was the
custom. The day their pastor resigned, the executive
committee of the church extended me a call.

I was afraid to accept. I knew that I did not have
much experience in the ministry and that I was not
as spiritually equipped as the former pastor.

In addition, all the members of the executive
committee were much older than I and all but one
had some type of executive position where they
were used to giving orders.

So I decided to make it nearly impossible for them
to accept me by laying down as my conditions for
coming at least three things the church had refused
to do for the former pastor. I can assure you that my
meeting with the board was interesting and long.
The committee gave in on one item, but persistently
tried to persuade me to give in on the remaining
conditions. Each time I would say, "Gentlemen, you

can do better in choosing a pastor and I would suggest some older and more experienced man." Then I would say, "I settled these conditions of coming before God, and before my session with you tonight. I do not wish to be stubborn or arbitrary, but I feel I cannot accept your call, though I am honored by the invitation to be your pastor."

By midnight, there remained just one point they had not accepted. "Now that we've gone so far and met you most of the way, you will certainly come."

"I'm sorry, men. I love every one of you and you are all my personal friends. I hope you will still love me, but I can't come."

It was as if a thunderbolt had hit the place. So I apologized again, expressed my concern that I had kept them up so late and praised them for their generosity in conceding so much. I said, "Good night and God bless you." That was another bombshell.

They asked if I would excuse myself again. Later, much later, they called me back and said, "We have decided you are God's man. Therefore, we have no choice but to meet all of your conditions."

I can assure you that as a young man of 25, God knew that with such a strong executive committee I would need that edge. So Dorothy, Richard and baby Daniel moved from Clarion and began their second pastorate in Meadville, Pennsylvania.

Soon after our arrival, there was an annual meeting with the election of officers. I sensed in just a few minutes that there was division in the camp. I called them the "Republicans and Democrats," because each group was vying for power and position. It became so vocal that I feared it would get out of control, so I said, "Would you all mind standing?" I pronounced the benediction and said carefully, so I could control myself, "You may all go home and when we can return and act like Christian ladies and gentlemen, we'll continue our election."

Before the opportunity came for another election, a crisis arose. The president of the bank that held the mortgage on our church asked me to come and see him. He started in on me directly. "Preacher, your people are dishonest. They have paid nothing on the principal or interest on their mortgage for over two years. Nobody has even dropped into the bank to see me or to talk about it. I am fed up. I want you to understand that when this mortgage comes due in three weeks, I expect you to make full payment of all the principal, past and present, and all the interest and the interest on the interest, and if you are one dollar short, I am selling your church."

I tried to explain that I was new, and that I knew nothing about this. I pleaded, "If you will be a little patient with us, I will see that everything is caught up."

Angrily and loudly he replied, "You have three weeks, and when it is due, I expect every dollar. If you are one dollar lacking, I will sell the church."

To say I was frightened is putting it mildly. I visited everybody I thought might have a dollar hidden under a mattress somewhere. But all my efforts were in vain. A week passed and all my streets had dead ends.

In desperation I went to my father in Erie. I sat in his study and explained everything, including what I thought would happen to my family and me if the church was sold.

Very calmly—too much so to suit me—my father said, "Son, if I were in your place, what do you think I would do?" Now, that was not what I wanted him to say. I wanted names, places, ways and means to obtain the money. Disgusted, I replied, "I suppose you'd get your Bible, go and fast and pray and expect God to give you a promise, and wait and see what He would do."

"That's right, Richard. That is exactly what I would do. Go and do it."

I left his study angry, disappointed and sorrowful. But I returned home to do it. When I got home I said to my wife, "I'm going to my study and I'm locking the door. I don't want to see or talk to anybody unless they are dying. I am staying there until I hear from God."

Locked in my study, I took my Bible and stretched myself out on the floor. I cried awhile at first, the tension was so great. Then the thought came—why don't you follow the instructions your father gave you when you entered the ministry?

"Son, this is your source of supply," he had said as he had held up his Bible. "There will never come a time, circumstance or need for guidance that the answer is not in the Bible. Learn to go to the book."

"Oh," I said to myself, "I'm reading in Second Chronicles. Those passages are full of jaw-breaking names."

The day before I had read 2 Chronicles 18, so I read the next chapter and felt no help there. But I had not gone very far into the 20th chapter when I discovered a man who was in even more trouble than I was. Not only was he going to lose his place of worship (the temple)—but his city, his country and his life.

What did Jehoshaphat do? I read and reread the chapter. I concluded it was a road map out of trouble and disaster. Since it had saved him from disaster so miraculously, I would follow step by step as accurately as possible the same procedure.

So I set myself to seek the Lord. I also called for the entire church to fast and pray all day the Sunday before the note was due. We would stay at the church during the noon time and all afternoon until the evening service. I determined I would put spiritual needs first and the last emergency we would pray about would be our financial pressure.

Probably no single event affected my future ministry as much as that one did. Here is a list of wonderful things God did in answer to prayer and fasting that Sunday:

1. The leaders of the rival groups got right with each other and at the next midweek service we had an orderly and smooth election of church officers.

2. Three young men received a call from God to the ministry during the prayer time.

3. In the middle of the afternoon a young man, who often at crucial times in the services had undergone an epileptic seizure, went into such a seizure and the entire congregation prayed for him. God

delivered him and as far as I know (I inquired of his brother some years later) he never had another attack.

4. At the close of the service I requested that whatever offering the people had for the church building debt be given to the church treasurer or financial secretary who would be standing by the door. When all had left the church, the two men came into the parsonage which was connected to the church and emptied the offering plates and their pockets on the dining room table. The offering was sufficient to pay the principal and interest, plus one dollar to spare.

5. But that was not all. The worst of the great depression of the thirties was on. Eighty-eight percent of my congregation was unemployed. That very next week all of my people got jobs. (We had prayed that afternoon for work for our unemployed.)

The Hookless Fastener Co. (the original zipper people) had their plant in our town and one of the managers was at our prayer time. The officials had heard of our day of fasting and prayer.

The orders started to come on Monday and kept coming all week. The employment office was instructed to hire anyone I sent up for a job. The management felt that orders were coming because our church had prayed. The news soon spread, "Join Harvey's church and you'll get a job!" I assure you the church was filled, and best of all, people were converted and it stayed full.

6. For six months we didn't have a fruitless Sunday

service. There was always an open response to the gospel invitation.

7. We enlarged our church building and paid for the construction as we went along.

8. Another result, I set a pattern for myself. No matter where I served as pastor after that, every six months, spring and fall, we observed a Sunday of fasting and prayer. More than any other single practice I had, I believe that fasting and prayer contributed most to any success that was observed in my pastorates.

Is any sick among you? Let him call the elders of the church; and let them pray over him, anointing him with oil in the name of the Lord; And the prayer of faith shall save the sick and the Lord shall raise him up. . . .

James 5:14–15a

17 Miracles at Meadville

One Sunday morning as I was on my way up the aisle to the platform, my beloved senior elder approached me. "Pastor, I would like to talk to you for a moment." I agreed and we started for the rear of the church. He then suggested that we go to my study.

Just inside the door, without any words of preparation, he said, "Richard, of late I have not enjoyed your preaching." My first reaction was to retort that my preaching was between me and my God and no one was going to tell me what I was going to preach. But the Holy Spirit checked me.

"Mr. B., I know I am a young man and I could be overly zealous and wrong, but you know me well; you know that I try to do nothing but the will of God. I will tell you what I am willing to do and I will ask you to do the same. I will refrain from eating dinner today and fast and pray until the evening service and you can be sure that I will do whatever God shows me." He agreed to do the same and we parted.

I had been preaching on sensational subjects and popular themes. The elder had come from a very conservative background and by former training was much opposed to some of the things I was doing.

For that evening I had announced my subject as the "Last Round Up." It was a popular song that was number one on the hit parade. Also, I had advertised that an outstanding singer would sing new words which had been composed to the tune by a local poet. I had received prior permission to do so from the publisher.

It rained hard all that Sunday and was still raining in the evening. Ordinarily, the crowd would have been much smaller than usual, as very few people had cars. After much prayer, reading of God's Word and meditating, I prayed, "Oh God, I am under pressure about my preaching and my heart is full of fear. My mind is confused and I am having difficulty discerning your voice. Please be patient with me. If I am truly following You and doing Your will, let me know by performing four things:

"1. Under the circumstances I'm liable to be all tied up in my preaching, so give me freedom and liberty as I preach about the judgment of God.

"2. This storm naturally will keep the people away. Please pack out the church tonight.

"3. Give me a dozen first-time professions of faith and please make more than half of them adults.

"4. Lord, you know my finances. I have bills far beyond any Sunday offerings I have received thus far. You know the ones I must pay tomorrow. So please give me the largest offering I have ever received." (I received no salary—the loose offerings made up my income.)

I went to my radio broadcast and returned just about the time the evening service was about to begin. I was a bit late because of the heavy rain. When I sat down on the platform I noticed that the church was full, even the vestibule.

There was just one vacant seat, in the front row, right in the center and directly before the pulpit. As I lifted my eyes from silent prayer my equilibrium was shaken. I watched the usher as he led the senior elder down the aisle to the empty seat. I cried to the Lord, "Only you can help me now."

Somehow I never seemed to see Mr. B. as I preached. God gave me both liberty and serenity.

When the invitation was given, 11 adults, eight of them men, and two high school young people responded.

And the offering was the largest I had received for many months and was sufficient to meet our needs. Neither Mr. B. nor I ever spoke of the matter of my preaching again.

On one of my visits to some very influential people in my church, the man of the house spoke up during our conversation. "Pastor, in no way am I trying to influence you. Nor do I object to you or any other minister speaking on baptism. But just so there is no misunderstanding between us, I want you to understand that my wife and I are both satisfied with our baptism when we were infants. As far as I am concerned, I never expect to be baptized again."

"If you are satisfied, that is the important thing," was my answer and the discussion ceased.

When June rolled around I thought it was time to have another baptismal service. There were quite a few new converts and since it was warmer weather, I chose to observe the ordinance Sunday afternoon in a nearby creek.

That Sunday morning I spoke about baptism, its meaning and how, in my opinion, immersion more accurately symbolized that meaning. On her way out of the church that morning the wife said, "Pastor, add my name to your list to be immersed this afternoon."

That woman had one of the largest goiters I have ever seen. It hung down almost to her chest and a physician had told her he did not think any surgeon would operate because it was so intertwined with all the nerves and blood vessels in her neck. In fact, surgery could have been fatal.

She must have told her husband of her plan to be baptized. Perhaps fearing that he might weaken and follow her into the water, he came to the baptismal service in his newest clothing and shoes. When it was her turn to be baptized, she was led out into the water by an elder.

While I was giving her instructions, from the shore came a booming voice. "Pastor, wait." The husband handed his watch to a friend. "Don't you want to give me your wallet too?" the friend asked. But the man just turned his head and remarked, "It needs baptizing too!"

So I baptized from head to toe the wife and man who had insisted the week before that they would never be immersed. As soon as they arrived home, the wife rushed into the bathroom, vomited up the goiter and was completely healed. Thus began a long succession of remarkable healings in the Meadville church.

Shortly after the above incident, I arrived home one afternoon from visiting some new families. In my living room sat the pastor of the First Baptist Church of Linesville, Pennsylvania, with one of his parishioners. As I entered the room, he stood up, introduced himself and the lady he had brought with him.

"I believe the Bible and know that God answers prayer in response to faith and heals people, but I don't have faith for this woman's healing. She has terminal cancer and the surgeon has just sent her home from Pittsburgh Presbyterian Hospital to take care of everything within a three-week period. She asked me to come and anoint and pray for her according to James chapter five. I have told her honestly that I do not have that kind of faith, but that I was willing to take her for prayer to anyone she thought might have it."

Then the lady said to me, "I have been listening to your radio broadcasts and you have been reporting healings in your church—here we are."

I turned to her. "Do you believe that if I pray for

you God will heal you?"

She answered tartly, "What do you think I am here for?"

I asked, "Do you believe the promises?" And I quoted James 5:14.

"I wouldn't have come if I hadn't believed it," was the snappy reply.

Taken aback by her replies and almost afraid to ask her any more questions, I said, "All right, kneel down here and we will anoint you with oil and pray for you." Turning to the pastor, I said, "The Bible says, 'If two of you agree as touching anything they shall ask, it shall be done for them by our Father which is in heaven.' Will you agree with me that this women should be healed and that Christ has the power to do so?"

"Oh yes," he replied.

We laid our hands on her, anointed her with oil and prayed for her.

The pastor took her home. She returned to bed. After a few days she felt herself sinking into unconsciousness. Everything was becoming black. She told me afterwards, "I cried out to Jesus, saying, 'I did what you told me to do and you said you'd heal me.' "

Then the Lord spoke to her as tartly as she had spoken to me and said, "If you believe, what are you doing in bed?"

"All right," she answered, "I'll get up."

As she proceeded to do so the blackness disappeared. By then, it was about time for her husband, a river boat captain, to come home for supper. She thought, "I'll start supper and greet him at the door." When she opened the door he was so shocked he fainted. His wife had to get a pitcher of water and throw it on his face to revive him. She was healed. I saw that woman 20 years later in good health, still testifying to the miraculous power of God.

Also at Meadville, one night at midnight there was a pounding at the front door. "Pastor, pastor." I got my bathrobe and practically slid down the banister. A young man stood at the door crying, "Mother is dying and is calling for you." I went upstairs two at a time, dressed and rushed down the stairs again. The young man started the car before I could shut the car door.

The Kaisers lived at the outer edge of town. We rushed into the house and found the mother rolled in a sheet, tossing, crying and sometimes screaming in pain.

I dropped by her bedside and prayed. I remained there, calling on God on her behalf for about an hour. The stench from her sickness began to affect me and I went into the next room to pace the floor and pray.

About 3:00 in the morning, the patient called for me to come to her bedside. "Pastor, I am about ready to die and I don't want to face Christ with the criticisms of you I have had in my heart and which I have voiced to others. Will you please forgive me?"

"Most certainly, I forgive you."

Then she hurriedly reached for a pail under the bed. It was a normal 10-quart galvanized pail. She began to gag and her face turned blue. Her husband pounded her on the back and tried to assist her. She pushed her thumb down her throat and pulled. And as she pulled, she brought up a cancer, roots and all. My guess is that she vomited a quart of cancer. The odor was terrible, but she was completely delivered.

Things were going well with me in Meadville. My congregation was growing, people were finding Christ, my income was on the increase. It may be that I was slackening in my spiritual fervor, God knows.

It was winter time, it was cold and there were flurries of snow in the air. My car would not start and I had to get to the broadcasting station where my father and I shared the responsibility of a program on alternate days. So I called a man and asked him to pick me up.

While I was waiting at the front window for his arrival, my new overcoat over my arm and my hat in my hand, I saw a flame of fire shoot out the door of the gas station across the street. Within the flames was a man screaming, "Help! Help!" The flames were shooting up into the air 12 or 15 feet.

I rushed out the front door and crossed the street yelling, "Lie down, roll, lie down, roll!" Finally the man did that just about the time I reached him. I tossed my new overcoat over him and extinguished the fire.

There was a telephone lineman up on a pole and when he saw what was happening, he connected his phone to a line and summoned an ambulance. By the time the fire was extinguished, the ambulance had arrived. They put the man, coat and all, on the stretcher and took off for the hospital with sirens blaring.

The fire victim was on his way to the hospital when my driver arrived to take me to the radio station. I confess it was hard to speak on that broadcast and I was anxious to get back and find out about the man.

Immediately upon my return to Meadville, I crossed to the gas station and inquired, "Who was that man?"

"Don't you know? Why he's the butcher across the street. Don't you buy your meat there?"

"Sure, I go there about three times a week. Where did they take him?"

When I found out, I went to the hospital. The sign on the door said, "Positively no visitors." I went to the desk and after an explanation was admitted.

Only four other people were admitted besides myself—the attending doctor and nurse and the wife and the priest. Having being burned over 80% of his body, the man died after four days.

Then God began to deal with me.

"Richard, you were not concerned about your coat. You willingly placed it on the man. You still don't know if it was damaged or if you will ever get it back."

"Who wouldn't give his coat to save a man's life?" I responded.

"But you visited that man's shop three times a week." The voice grew softer. "You never talked to him about his soul. You were more concerned about his body than about that which lives forever."

Then I realized that that man's blood was upon my hands. I had never sought to win him to Christ. I cried to God for forgiveness and mercy. But that man with his cries for help has disturbed my complacency ever since.

So it was that I set out to visit every home within a mile radius of the church. First, I left a tract and Gospel of John, explaining the way of salvation at every door.

Then I visited a second time and knocked on the door, attempting to tell everyone how to find God. Where there seemed to be interest, I visited for the third time.

I have never been the same minister of the gospel since. The fire incident is one of the causes of the inner drive I have this day to tell others God's Good News.

. . . but stand thou still a while, that I may show thee the word of God.

1 Samuel 9:27

18 Don't Preach!

My father retired from the ministry at the age of 69 years and nine months. The Sunday he resigned, the executive committee of the church at Erie, Pennsylvania, extended me a call through the district superintendent. I made an appointment to meet them. I never met with a more discouraged group of men. The depression had been on for about five years. Still over half of the congregation was out of work.

To the surprise of the executive committee, I laid down conditions that threw consternation into the group. "Men, I can only come if you tear down this building and build a larger church." They all gave me reasons why this was impossible. Of course, the biggest reason was money. Others said, "Let's fill the building we have first."

"Men, if I pay off the second mortgage and get permission from the person holding the first mortgage to rebuild, will you vote 'Yes'?"

They answered affirmatively, provided we would not go further into debt. I consented to accept the call. And I said, "It all depends on you here tonight. Let's take a 30-day pledge of how much you will give to clear the second mortgage." As nearly as I remember, the second mortgage was close to $4,000. I passed out slips of paper and said, "Write on this how much you feel you can give."

They pledged $1,300. The following Sunday, I obtained a substitute for my church in Meadville for the morning service. I went to Erie to preach and attempted to raise the balance. After that service I had $2,900. I put $100 with it and took the $3,000 to the lady who held the second mortgage.

"Would you accept $3,000 for the second mortgage?"

"No," was the emphatic reply.

I stood up, walked to her dining room table and began to count out one-hundred-dollar bills before her. When I had reached 30, I started to count them over again, and began to talk to her as I laid them down. "In this great depression, by great effort, I have raised this amount and it is all I can get. It will be a long, long time before you get this paid, if ever, under present conditions." Then I explained what I had hoped to do, but that it was possible only if she accepted the $3,000.

Without saying a word, she disappeared for a few minutes. When she returned, she laid the second mortgage on the table, marked it paid, picked up the money and left me standing there, happy and grateful.

We burned the second mortgage and raised $1,500 to start the new building. My parents, from an inheritance, gave me the first $1,000. It truly was a miracle in a city where building activity had practically ceased.

Almost every person in the church gave 100 hours of free labor. At every point of progress we held a Sunday afternoon rally. I brought in a speaker and a guest musician and we took a pledge offering. Thus we paid our bills as we built.

We had agreed on Saturday as the payday for the hired help. Many Saturdays when the day started, there was no money. You might have found the pastor behind the cement sacks desperately calling on God for help. At times the help did not arrive until the clock struck 12 noon. But not once did we have to say to a man, "We will pay you next week."

The Erie Gospel Tabernacle had the largest Sunday evening service in the city except for Easter and Christmas. It disturbed me that I lost some of my congregation on those important nights. I prayed and I thought. Then I hit on the idea of using visual sermons. I tried it; it worked. The crowds came and many were saved.

In the middle of my seven and a half years in Erie, I conducted an eight-day campaign of my own with guest musicians. God gave us 31 couples who professed Christ as Savior, and at the end of that year 25 of those couples were still in the church. Some of them, and later some of their children, entered the ministry. This group was known at the church as the "chain gang" because each couple brought another until we had whole rows of them—a marvelous sight to see.

One night I was preaching a prophetic sermon. I must have been long-winded. The people began to look at their watches and to turn around to see the clock on the back wall. That was too much!

I stopped preaching and held up my hands in a gesture of prayer. "Oh God," I cried out, "stop that clock!" It stopped. The altar was lined with seekers who saw what happened. For two weeks the caretaker would not start it because people were coming to see the clock that God had stopped in answer to prayer.

One summer I attended the Beulah Beach summer conference. The evening evangelist took seriously ill and informed the camp director that he would not be able to preach that Saturday evening.

Immediately the director searched the grounds for a substitute. Most of the preachers had gone home to fill their pulpits on Sunday. In desperation he came to this young man, Richard Harvey. "Could you help me out? Would you preach for me tonight?"

I was frightened, but I promised I would do my best. The thought came to me: "What would I preach about if it were the last sermon I would ever give?" My conclusion: the second coming of Christ, a message of warning. Thus I preached to my first conference crowd on Christ's coming, and the altar was filled across the full width of the tabernacle and into the first row of seats.

The next day when I met the conference director, he said, "Richard, would you be willing to be our youth evangelist next year?" I replied affirmatively.

During the intervening year I presented several very successful visual sermons. So I decided to use one of them every other day at conference and on the final Saturday, I would give the one I thought was most effective.

The crowds at the youth meetings grew every morning until by the end of the week standing room was at a premium. All week I had been publicizing the final Saturday morning's visual message.

At about 3:00 a.m. that final Saturday, I was wakened from a sound sleep. A voice, to me it seemed audible, said, "Don't preach this morning." I lay awake awhile thinking I was hearing things. I went back to sleep. About 4:00 a.m. I was wakened again. The voice very clearly said again, "Don't preach this morning."

I answered the voice, "Then what do I do?" I got no answer except the repetition of the voice saying, "Don't preach."

Scared and trembling, I lay there. My trembling wakened my wife. "What's the matter with you?" she asked.

"I'll tell you in the morning, go to sleep." I dozed off, but about daybreak I was again wakened with, "Don't preach this morning."

The crowd that gathered for the meeting would be hard to describe. There were people occupying every seat and every possible standing space, both inside and outside the summer youth tabernacle. The service started at 8:00 a.m. The promised visual sermon was constructed on the platform for all to see. I sat through all the preliminaries, not knowing what I was going to do or say, but knowing that four times I had been instructed not to preach. Nervous, I sat until introduced.

When I went to the pulpit, I said, "Young people, I feel that right now there is someone who must find Christ. Would you please step out and come forward?" Immediately a young man about 20 years old, who was right in the middle of the tabernacle, arose, pushed his way down the aisle and knelt at the altar. As soon as his knees hit the floor, someone else got up and came. And then one at a time people kept coming until the altar was filled.

We cleared the front seats and the process started again—people coming, one at a time, until the three sets of seats at the front were filled as well. Then it shut off as if someone had turned a faucet.

The meeting had started at 8:00 a.m., the coming to the altar at 8:30. It lasted till noon.

From that memorable service until now, I have never lacked for invitations to pastorates, evangelistic meetings or summer conferences. God sanctioned my ministry without preaching or any effort on my part. It was simply mine to obey!

Unto them that look for Him shall He appear the second time without sin unto salvation.

Hebrews 9:28

19 The Dream

There has been a controversy in my mind as to whether I should include this in my life story, but since it has had a strong motivating influence upon my life and ministry, I feel it necessary.

I have seen it in print, written by another. I have also heard two other speakers use the story as their own.

It could be that God gave the same dream or impression or vision or whatever it might be called to others also. But in the last 20 years I have related the experience only once or twice, not wishing to be accused of plagiarizing. Also, because of the doctrinal implication in the story, I must say that I felt the incident is like a parable that teaches one major truth and does not necessarily have to be in every part of a theological treatise.

And now, because of the lasting impression this dream has had upon my ministry, I venture to put it into print.

I had been working very long hours as a pastor—many days 14–17 hours.

The annual legislative gathering of our society was holding its meeting in Asheville, North Carolina. Rather than lodge in the main convention hotel, my wife and I decided to seek a more restful place out in the hills around Asheville. In a beautiful spot we found a secluded cabin and rented it.

On the way back from the evening service one night, we looked for a snack before retiring but neither of us found what we wanted. We went to bed not having had anything to eat since our evening meal. This dream, therefore, was not the result of mince pie, hot dogs or onions!

In my sleep I heard the phone ring. I answered. It was one of the leading men in our church. "Pastor, I just woke up and my wife is gone. I find no signs that she has dressed, nor are any of her clothes gone."

"Let me do some phoning and I'll call you back."

Before I had the opportunity to dial, the phone rang again. When I answered, I heard the hysterical voice of one of the young women in my congregation. "Pastor, my mother and father are not here. There is no sign of a struggle. Even the bedclothes are not rumpled and their clothing is undisturbed. Have you any idea where they might be?"

"I'll phone you right back."

As the receiver clicked, my phone rang again. "Richard."

"Yes."

"I'm the neighbor next door to your father and mother. The lights have been on for hours, so Jack and I thought we had better see if there was trouble of some kind. But when we went over, your mother and father were not there. Everything else at the house seemed to be normal."

By now, I was beginning to come to a conclusion. "Oh, I think I know where they are. I'll call back within the hour."

My wife and I were still present and so was our entire family, securely sleeping in their beds. I called a few families in the church and all but one was in shock. I hated to admit it to myself, but I was certain that the Lord Jesus had come, the missing ones had been taken, and that I had been left behind. His word was, "Unto them that look for Him shall He appear the second time." I had been too busy and too active in my church work to be anticipating His return. I believed in His coming, I preached about it once in a while, but the cares of this world and some of its "things" were uppermost in my thoughts and plans!

The next day was Sunday. I was surprised at the number of people present at the service. I was also surprised to see who was missing. Hesitantly, one of my parishioners asked, "Pastor, why are you still here?"

Caught with the goods, I made a public confession of my lukewarmness of heart.

What would happen next? I did not have long to wait.

Everything seemed normal as Monday morning dawned. It being just after the first of the month, my utility bills needed to be paid. There was also the usual list of groceries to buy.

I decided to go to the electric company first. I placed the bill and money on the counter. The girl looked at me and said, "Reverend Harvey, would you please let me see your left hand? I see you have not received the official seal. Here are the places where you can obtain it." Then she handed me a card. "You have 48 hours or we will turn off the power."

"Thank you." I walked slowly out of the building. I hoped this would not apply to the water company, but it did. The seriousness of the situation began to dawn on me.

What were we going to do? Where could I go? Would I see my children starve?

I got into the car and headed for home. I thought, "At least I can get the groceries because the grocer and his family are members of my church."

But when I entered the door of the grocery store, Mollie (the clerk) raised her arms toward the ceiling and screamed, "Oh pastor, I just knew you'd come this morning and how was I going to tell you that I couldn't sell you any more groceries? You have heard what has happened, haven't you?"

"Yes, I've heard. I just thought maybe the proclamation had not reached the small retail stores yet."

The owner stepped out from his office at the rear. "Pastor, I am very sorry. Since I can't sell you anything, I'll tell you what I will do. Just after dark, go to the rear of the building and under the back steps you will find two baskets of groceries—just take them as a love gift from all of us. Leave us your list and we'll try and see that those items are included."

I thanked him and left.

"I'd better get my gas tank filled," I thought, and stopped at the gasoline station across the street from our home. The owner was a good friend and I had attempted to leave a clear witness about Christ down through the years.

"Fill it up," I asked as he emerged.

"Preacher, you know I can't. I know you have no mark, I'd be disappointed in you if you did. You don't have it, do you?"

"No, I don't."

"Preacher, I've already thought about what I'd do in this situation. After closing hours, on my way home, I'll drop off a couple of five-gallon cans of gas and a case of oil beside your garage."

"Thanks so much." And I started for home.

I sat in front of the house for a while, wondering how I would relate the events of the morning to my wife and what I would say to the three children.

As I opened the car door my second son, David, came running, "Dad, Dad, my team just beat Dan's! We won big." Then Dan came running and I took them both into the house.

"Boys, I want to explain something to you. We are going to have to leave our lovely home and find some deserted place in the woods and try to survive. We just can't take 'the mark.' Do you understand what I mean?"

"Yes, Dad. We know what you mean, and if necessary, we'll die with you and Mom."

I hugged them. "I'll talk to Mom and we'll decide what essential things we'll take with us."

At the foot of the stairs my three-year-old daughter, Marilyn, came running and jumped into my arms. Her curls caressed my face. I hugged her tightly as I dared. "How, oh how, can I explain to her?" I agonized. "How can I stand to hear her cry for food?"

"Oh God, please help me now," I cried. Then I burst into tears. I literally, actually did. My sobbing woke my wife. She shook me, "What's wrong with you?"

In my sleepy, hazy state I said, "Oh, I just had a terrible dream. I'll tell you about it in the morning." I lay awake the rest of the night thinking about what had happened in the dream.

"God," I prayed, "I wouldn't be left behind, would I?" The only answer that came was the Scripture, "Unto them that look for Him shall He appear the second time without sin unto salvation" (Hebrews 9:28). "Watch . . . that ye may be accounted worthy to escape all these things that shall come to pass, and to stand before the Son of man" (Luke 21:36).

20 The Check for St. Louis

I was away from home in an evangelistic series when the Lord spoke to me in the night. "You are going to have a son who will minister to me in troubled times." The next morning I wrote my wife telling her what I felt. She replied that I must have eaten something the night before! But by the time I arrived home, she knew that there would be an addition to the family. (Already the Lord had given us a daughter, Marilyn, in Erie.)

My wife's doctor, a famous obstetrician, told her he was certain she would have a daughter, and that he had seldom been wrong in his predictions. Thus, he and I had a running debate over the matter. "Doctor," I said to him one day on a visit to his office, "if I were a betting man, I would bet all I have in this world that this baby will be a boy."

"How can you be so positive?"

"Well, doctor, I don't think I can explain it to your satisfaction, but I know."

God gave us our third son, John, January 2, 1942.

Near the end of seven years in Erie, I felt God was

saying that He wanted me to move. I didn't want to do it. The Erie church was peculiarly my church. Everyone, with few exceptions, had come into the church either under my father's ministry or mine. I tried at first to ignore the impressions of the Holy Spirit to my heart. Then God began to speak louder and through the force of circumstances.

I was asked by a district superintendent, H.E. Nelson, to candidate in St. Louis. I told him I had no interest in moving there. When I went and saw the situation, I had less interest.

They had no building of their own but met in a rented church basement. They didn't even own their own chairs or songbooks. There was no parsonage and only a very small congregation.

I thanked them for their kindness in considering me, but told them I wasn't interested. To the district superintendent who had asked me to go, I wrote a burning letter. "What could you be thinking of, asking me to consider such a group?" I demanded. I had individual Sunday school classes in Erie many times the size of that entire congregation!

The superintendent ignored the letter. The St. Louis church extended me a call and the superintendent approved it.

The next week, a traveling salesman took me to lunch. "I understand you have been to St. Louis."

"Yes," I replied disgustedly.

"Harvey, if you'll go there, I'll personally pay for a radio broadcast for you for six months."

I didn't even say "thank you." Inside I was angry because I knew God was putting the pressure on.

"Well, I'll let you know if I go, but don't lose any sleep over it."

I went to Minneapolis for a two-week evangelistic effort. In the mornings we had Bible studies on faith, the Holy Spirit and the Christian's daily walk. One morning Bible study was on the subject of obedience and as I was speaking, God said to me, "You are not practicing what you preach." I paused, thinking everyone there must have heard.

The pause was so long I felt the audience needed an explanation. So I told them what it was all about—the controversy between God and me, and why I didn't want to go to St. Louis. I ended my explanation saying, "There isn't even a place to live! No parsonage, and besides that, there isn't a house to rent in the city." Laughingly I added, "And as for buying, imagine a poor preacher buying a house!"

Two nights later, the host pastor's telephone rang just after midnight. Next morning at the breakfast table, the pastor inquired if I had heard it. I admitted that I had.

"Mr. Harvey, I never experienced anything like last night. The call was from a lady who has only recently come to our church. She is a neighbor of one of our members. She asked that my wife and I come to her home right away as she might change her mind about what she had to do if she waited till morning. She said she was sure God was directing her.

"When we arrived, there were no introductions nor preliminary conversation. 'Rev. C., here is a check for $1,000 for foreign missions. I know your church is very interested in that.' Then she handed me another check for $1,000. 'This is for the new building you are constructing.' She disappeared for a minute and then returned with her checkbook saying, 'This is for the evangelist as a down payment on a house in St. Louis. He said God is telling him to go there and no house can be rented.'

"It was a strange figure for a gift—$643.37." (That figure may not be exactly accurate to the penny, but it definitely was a strange and irregular amount.)

I was stunned and unhappy. Now I knew I had to go to St. Louis. I immediately excused myself from the table and wrote out my resignation to the Erie church. I then phoned the acting chairman of the St. Louis group, accepted the call and requested that he have a Christian realtor meet me at the airport at Lambert Field, Monday morning, at a given hour.

The realtor was there to greet me. Almost immediately after shaking hands he said, "I have contacted nearly every realtor I know and they all say the same thing, 'There is just not a house to rent here.' "

"All right, let's look at some houses with the idea of buying." Every house Mr. Finke took me to see had something wrong with it. Finally we pulled up in front of a fine house on Westminster Avenue.

"I want to explain about this house. First of all, the tenant will not allow anyone on the inside. But I have reason to believe it is just as nice on the inside as on the outside."

"How much is it?"

"Well, before we discuss money, let me tell you

about the government's requirements. (The house had been reclaimed on a government loan.) It is necessary for you to have the loan payment. By that I mean that you must sign that you have not borrowed it from any lending institution or any friend or relative. You are a Christian, so I know you will not sign unless it is the entire truth."

"How much is the down payment?"

"$643.37."

I reached into my pocket and pulled out the check for that exact amount. I turned it over, endorsed it and handed it to Mr. Finke.

The house was all I had hoped it to be.

> *Except a corn of wheat fall into the ground and die,
> it abideth alone; but if it die, it bringeth forth much
> fruit.*
>
> John 12:24

21 Mansion Blues

When we moved to St. Louis, Missouri, we had a new son, an 80% cut in income and the inflationary prices of World War II with which to contend. The church was small and met in a rented basement. The draft began to take the leading married men and the congregation dwindled. New people were not coming as quickly as the older members left. I tried not to show my discouragement either at home or at the church, but the lack of growth and progress was getting to me.

I began to look for a better location.

Soon I found a building for sale at Lindell and Kingshighway just across from beautiful Forest Park. It was a big white stone mansion with 26 rooms, six bathrooms, three floors and an elevator. I sought out the realtor. He told me the house was up for public bid and that within 60 days the bids would be opened, the highest bidder getting the property.

When I submitted a bid of $12,550, the realtor

laughed, "Son, that wouldn't buy the front entrance or the fireplace in the library." He didn't want to accept the bid. I insisted and gave him an earnest check for $500.

I prayed, "God, if you want me to have it, keep anyone else from bidding." That is exactly what happened. My bid was the only one.

After some remodeling, the Harvey family moved in on the second floor. The two parlors on the first floor were made into a chapel.

Little did I know the trouble I was in for! We were in the elite section of St. Louis. Many old-line families, political leaders and business giants lived in that six-block section. They didn't want a church in their private domain.

First they threatened me personally, then sent the police and then the sheriff to notify me that I could not hold church services there. Before buying the property I had checked and the zoning permitted a church there although the deed restrictions specified a one-family dwelling.

I continued to maintain a full church program. The pressure grew. The neighbors stirred up the labor unions to picket the place, as we were using our own labor to remodel inside.

I took coffee and soft drinks to the picketers and that made my neighbors even angrier.

For a while new people were afraid to come. It got so that my wife dreaded to answer the door bell for fear it might be another law officer with some court order or summons.

In spite of all these court actions and publicity the

church grew some, but very slowly, and then seemed to drop again.

I became more discouraged. Nothing I did seemed to help. I wanted to die. I even prayed, "Oh Lord, give me pneumonia!" No such respite.

On one occasion in desperation I walked against the traffic light at one of St. Louis' busiest corners. Brakes screamed, drivers leaned out of windows and cursed me. "Why didn't you hit me?" I yelled.

My discouragements grew larger and the congregation smaller. Every week the attendance dropped. I became desperate. God wasn't hearing me. Nothing I tried to do worked, but I was afraid to quit.

In desperation I sought the woods in the center of Forest Park and screamed out to God. Finally, I confessed the pride in my heart. I had thought I could do it. I confessed the rebellious spirit I had against God. "Oh God, if what You want is for me to preach to 12 people, lift me above all this and help me. I'll even preach to 12."

Next Sunday there were 12.

After the service my wife said to me, "Richard, what has happened to you? This is the first good sermon I've heard you preach in six months."

"Oh, the Lord and I just had it out."

The attendance grew a little, my spirit rose, but the pressures continued to mount. Many times I still felt crushed.

I see now that I had to be broken. But out of the rubble of my brokenness a whole new ministry emerged.

Behold, I will do a new thing; now it shall spring forth; shall ye not know it?

Isaiah 43:19a

22 Birth of Youth for Christ

One day in the fall of 1943, I stood on the corner of Eighth and Olive Streets in downtown St. Louis. The high school nearby had just let out. As hundreds of young people crossed the street in front of me, God spoke to my heart, "I'm going to hold you accountable for these young people."

I argued with God. "They won't come to my church, nor will they listen to my radio program."

But from that moment, the responsibility for the souls of the youth of that city came down upon me. I cried out for them at night and was so troubled during the day that I could think of nothing but those young people on their way to hell.

About two weeks later I received a letter from Roger Malsbury of Indianapolis asking me to speak in that city at a Saturday night youth rally called Youth for Christ. I learned that there were at that time at least six such rallies being held in the United States. The best known was the Word of Life in New York City and the Voice of Christian Youth in Detroit, both of which had been in existence for some time.

God truly inspired me at the Indianapolis rally. He gave me a plan as to how it could be done in St. Louis. I returned home to pray and work.

I gathered together 50 Christian laymen and a group of ministers from as many denominations as possible advisors. We rented Kiel Auditorium for Saturday nights. I appeared before ministerial associations, explaining our plans and purposes. To my surprise, most of them gave me their endorsement and blessing.

Dr. R.G. Lee of Memphis, Tennessee, was our first speaker and the Jackie Burros musical team took part in the program.

The first night the smaller auditorium was crowded out and by actual count there were 1,100 turned away. Many found the Lord Jesus as Savior on that opening night. We were on our way! We moved into a larger auditorium from then on. A low attendance would be 1,500, and a really good one, 3,500. The average was about 2,000.

I began to feel that all big cities should have a rally. I went to Chicago and inquired as to who might be the most upcoming young preacher in the city at the time. "Torrey Johnson" was the usual answer, so I sought him out. I explained what was being done in St. Louis and invited him to come and speak at our rally. He came and brought Bev Shea and Doug Fischer as soloist and pianist. That night over 3,000 attended.

Within a few weeks the National Association of Evangelicals convention was meeting in Columbus,

Ohio, and I was scheduled to be there.

At the NAE convention there were hundreds of copies of a new religious paper called *Protestant Voice*. Two weeks before a reporter and a photographer had been sent by the paper to our St. Louis rally. The two inside pages were filled with pictures—the crowds, the many servicemen in attendance, the seekers for God. The story of the beginning of Youth for Christ in St. Louis took up much of the edition.

The chairman of the convention asked me to take 20 minutes to tell the delegates about our rallies. When I finished, I was besieged by pastors from all over America.

Torrey Johnson got hold of me. "Dick, come to the hotel with me and let's go over every detail of how you do this." When Torrey arrived back in Chicago, he began immediately to set up his own committee. In less than two months after the NAE convention, 50 to 75 Youth for Christ rallies were begun.

Later, while visiting with Torrey, he expressed concern, "Dick, these rallies are bearing our name and some are not doing well. Some are conducted in a manner which could bring reproach to Christ. Let's organize a national committee and get it on a good footing." Thus five men officially incorporated Youth for Christ International—three ministers (Torrey Johnson, Richard Harvey and Robert Cook) and two laymen.

Within a month we felt we had overstepped our bounds, so we wrote each group inviting them to an organizational meeting at the Cadillac Hotel in

Detroit. About 35 came. The original officers of the incorporation were elected in a formal setting.

It was decided that a still more representative convention should be held. Again, at Winona Lake conference grounds, a complete election took place. Dr. Torrey Johnson was elected president and Richard Harvey, vice-president.

By the end of the first year of rallies in St. Louis, more than 900 had professed conversion. Their names and addresses were turned over to local churches, and over 300 people applied to colleges for preparation for Christian service.

After three years as the St. Louis Youth for Christ director and first vice-president of Youth for Christ International, I felt it necessary to resign. The local church was suffering greatly in many areas and needed more of my time.

The St. Louis YFC was left in the qualified hands of Bill Weston, who continues there until this day. Billy Graham was chosen first vice-president of YFC International.

I waited patiently for the Lord, and he inclined unto me, and heard my cry.

Psalm 40:1

23 Preacher, Sit Down!

After five years of legal manoeuvering, the judge finally informed us we could no longer hold services in the Lindell Avenue mansion.

A former lodge building on the south side of St. Louis was put on the market for $55,000. It was an excellent opportunity. Terms were $5,000 down and $50,000—30 days later.

Our congregation had a season of fasting and prayer and after much sacrificial giving and many outside gifts, $5,000 was raised. But we had to secure $50,000 in cash within 30 days. It was due on Good Friday, no later than 5:00 p.m. If we failed, the $5,000 would be forfeited.

Although every avenue was tried, we seemed to make no progress in those 30 days. Each effort met with a dead end. Our only hope was a loan from First National Bank if I could produce enough collateral. And that proved impossible.

Good Friday came. I was at the First National Bank at 9:00 a.m., opening time, and went immediately to the office of the vice-president.

Once again I explained my plight. He informed me that although he would like to assist me, it was entirely impossible because I could not meet government requirements for collateral.

I thanked him for his interest and the efforts he had made on my behalf and started to leave.

"Preacher, sit down!" He went through all the reasons why he could not possibly loan the church the money. Again, I started to leave. That time I got to the door. He called me back, excused himself, took care of another customer, and I waited.

Noon time came. He called me over to him during the lunch hour, then excused himself, and went to talk the situation over with the president. Again the verdict came back, "I'm sorry, but we'd be in trouble with the bank examiner."

I suggested he call my former banker in Erie, Pennsylvania. After his call he said, "Sir, that's the greatest recommendation I have ever heard given to a man, and he promised to put it in writing. I don't believe I could receive one as good as that myself." I was curious as to what my former banker had said that was so good, so I asked, "Would you mind telling me what he said?"

" 'Whatever Mr. Harvey promises you, he will do. You can depend on that, unless he dies! I would trust him with any amount within reason if I were satisfied with the terms of promised payment.' "

We sat and discussed the amount of the payments. I told him that we would pay a certain amount on the principal the first year, so much the second year and third year and also that I would not resign or leave the city without the bank being satisfied on all financial matters.

Again the vice-president discussed the loan with the president. Hope began to rise within me, only to have it dashed when he returned saying the bank would be in trouble with the government inspectors. It was closing time.

I thanked him for his day of effort on our behalf and rose to leave. "Young man, sit down." He went into a long explanation about how terrible he felt to turn me away when my church would have no place to worship on Easter Sunday morning.

Once more he excused himself, requesting that I remain until he returned. I was afraid to leave. My wife knew only that I had gone to the bank at 9:00 a.m. She was at home trying to pacify members of the congregation who wanted to find out if we would be able to obtain the lodge building and what about their $5,000 deposit and where would we hold church on Easter Sunday?

It was 4:30 p.m. when he came back to his office. Again he told me how sorry he was that the bank could not loan me the money. Once again I started to thank him and leave. Again he asked me to sit down. He sat and stared and said nothing.

The five o'clock hour was fast approaching. We were about to lose $5,000. I finally broke the silence and said, "Sir, I've got to go. I have an appointment at the realtor's." I arose.

"I can't see you on the street or in the park on Easter Sunday. This is Good Friday and I should do a good deed. I'll take the personal risk and answer the bank examiners and the bank board myself." He sat down and wrote out a check for $50,000 and handed it to me. It was 4:50 p.m. I thanked him and literally ran the few blocks to the realtor's office, arriving as his clock reached 5:00 p.m. The deal was consummated, the keys turned over.

Our longest and most trying ministry, nine years of St. Louis, ended. It was one of our most effective ministries, far-reaching as far as the whole church of Jesus Christ was concerned.

I wouldn't take anything for the experiences, but neither would I want them over again!

Precious in the sight of the Lord is the death of his saints.

Psalm 116:15

24 Mother and Dad Cross Over

It was during the pressure days of the early forties that both my father and mother went to be with the Lord. Mother went first. When she died, father was physically unfit to care for the closing of the estate. My brothers, Earl and Lynn, lived some distance away in California and Texas respectively, and so the responsibility was mine.

Father decided to sell both the property and contents of the house. The house, barn and acreage went easily; the rest was to go by auction.

Mother and father had lived their final years together on the old homestead of my mother's parents in Conneaut, Ohio. The sprawling farm house on Route 20 had accumulations from about three generations which, it seemed, had never disposed of a thing. Oh, to get rid of a hundred years of accumulation! The attic was filled with "unmentionables"; not even a corset was ever thrown away. I decided to burn them all.

A great pile of junk was stacked in the back yard, the fire set, and then, suddenly, I saw a roll of dollar bills emerge from a burning corset! I extinguished the fire in record time. Going through the remains of unburned underthings, I discovered almost $300 sewn in the garments. How much burned? The thought disturbs me still.

The night after the experience, I was trying to sleep in a bedroom on the second floor and having a hard time of it. The fire experience plus the $160 we had found in books on the shelves bothered me. I had given away over half the books before I discovered money in them.

My uncle, who had lived with my grandparents before my parents moved into the house, did not trust banks. I discovered tin cans stuffed in rafters as well as under floor boards, all containing various sums of money.

As I thought about all of this, my eyes focused on my grandmother's old button box. I had played with it as a child. It contained hundreds of buttons of all sizes and shapes. Some may have been two centuries old. I had enjoyed running my fingers through them.

An urge came to do it again. I got out of bed, picked up the box and started to run my fingers through the buttons. I hit something. I tried again. Whatever it was, it moved. After three or four attempts it surfaced, and I found a roll of 14 twenty-dollar bills.

Minutes before my mother had drawn her last breath, she had called me to her side. I tried with my ears and eyes to understand what she was trying to tell me; there was something she wanted me to find, but what, I never learned.

She then called my older brother, who was out of fellowship with the Lord and very heavy on my parents' hearts. With her remaining strength she pulled him down to her, hugged him tightly, whispered and wept. And then she was gone.

Mother had no insurance, so the money found throughout the house cared for her funeral expenses. We sold the antiques for a pittance. Today the value would run into the thousands. Many pieces were rare and perfect. I wish I had been older and wiser.

My father, age 81, returned with us to St. Louis and lived a year with us there. His godly life was a benediction to our family and to all who came in contact with him.

One day when I saw he was feeling a little stronger than usual I asked, "Dad, would you like to go calling with me this afternoon?"

"Yes, son, I would."

At the first home where we stopped, a five-year-old boy answered the door bell. His eyes caught those of my father, and he went running. "Mommy, Mommy, come quick! Jesus is standing at the door!"

"He can't be," admonished the mother.

"But he is, Mother. Come and see."

I looked at my father's face. His eyes were soft, tender and sympathetic, and his face had the shine of heaven on it. I understood what the child meant.

After a year with us in St. Louis, Father felt he should spend some time with Earl in California. I secured a bedroom on the train for him, tipped the porter well, and my father headed west.

Dad's health deteriorated very rapidly and he was soon under 24-hour care. I made one visit to see him and was shocked at his complete deterioration. He could hold an intelligent conversation for only a few minutes, but when he prayed, he was as clear mentally and as inspired as he ever was.

One day I received a letter from my brother. "Dad is in the hospital and failing very rapidly, but please don't come until I send for you." He promised to give me sufficient time to make the journey. The day his letter arrived, I went calling on parishioners, but couldn't keep my mind off my father.

An urge inside kept getting stronger and stronger.

"Go see your father, go see your father now!" I shoved it to the back of my mind, saying to myself, "It's just a son's love exerting itself and don't forget, Earl especially said, 'Don't come until I send for you.'" But the urge became too strong to resist. I went home and made reservations on the evening train.

In the midwest, I telephoned my brother.

"Where are you?" he asked.

"In Nebraska, on my way." Did that create a storm!

"Didn't I tell you not to come yet?"

"Yes, you told me, but I had to come. All this is costing me money. Meet me at such and such a city at such a time," and I hung up. He met me all right, but with the fury an older brother reserves for the younger who hasn't taken his advice. For 88 miles, he bawled me out.

As we approached the city of Merced, which was Earl's residence, he said, "Well, do you wish to go to the house first to freshen up or go to the hospital now?"

"I came to see Father. Let's go straight to the hospital."

If my brother had not taken me to Father's bedside, I would never have recognized him. When I had seen him last, he had weighed about 160 pounds. Now there was nothing left but a skeleton with skin pulled over it—60 pounds or less. His eyes were sunk deep into his head, he was paralyzed from the hips upward and unconscious as far as anyone could determine. And he had been that way for three weeks.

"Oh God," I cried within, "why did you send me here to see my father like this?"

I called for the nurse. "My father is dying, isn't he?"

"I don't know," she answered evasively.

"Then get me someone who can tell me."

"I'll send for the doctor."

When the doctor arrived, I asked the doctor the same question, "My father is dying, isn't he, Doctor?"

"Yes, Mr. Harvey, he is."

I was sure of it. His eyes were set and glassy, the death dew was on his brow, foam was gathered on his lips and the death rattle was in his throat. I reached under the covers and took hold of his hand. It was cold and clammy, and his nails were black.

Memories flooded my mind of days at home. I thought of the advice, counsel and loving help he had given me, yet now he didn't even know I was there.

All at once he sat up in bed. He had not moved a muscle for weeks. He pulled his hand away from mine and took his other hand from under the covers. He raised his arms toward the ceiling, his eyes and head turned heavenward. The expression on his face changed rapidly. Those blank eyes became expressive. One could see amazement, glory, ecstasy on his countenance.

The nursing supervisor began motioning for the people in the large ward to come near. Others came in from the hall as they passed the ward's big double doors. Soon a crowd had gathered to watch my father die. His face shone like someone had put a thousand-watt light bulb inside. His countenance was so bright it was hard to look directly into his face. For at least five minutes, and possibly longer, silence reigned as we all gazed into the face of a dying saint. All at once he seemed to lurch upward, then fell back. His spirit was gone.

The supervisor of nurses said, "I have been a nurse for 43 years. I've seen hundreds of people die, but I've never seen anyone die like this."

My brother turned to me, "Dick, heaven must be a far greater and more wonderful place than we have ever dreamed it to be. You could see the wonder and amazement on Father's face."

"For since the beginning of the world men have not heard, nor perceived by the ear, neither hath the eye seen, O God, beside thee, what he hath prepared for him that waiteth for him" (Isaiah 64:4).

> *Do the work of an evangelist, make full proof of thy ministry.*
>
> 2 Timothy 4:5

25 Jefferson Park

Many efforts were made to sell the mansion at 5035 Lindell Boulevard in St. Louis, but because of the deed restrictions and the court injunction it seemed everyone was afraid to buy it. I felt I could not leave St. Louis until it was sold. Only by its sale could the financial pressure on the church be lifted.

One Sunday morning five men walked into the sanctuary. Although they did not sit together, any pastor would have known that he was being "spied upon" by a pulpit committee from some church. At the close of the service they requested an interview and asked if I was willing to come to Chicago sometime to preach for them.

Arrangements were made. I really did not expect a call, but if one was extended, how could I possibly accept? Following the Sunday service, the executive committee of the independent Jefferson Park Bible Church asked for a session.

As was my lifelong custom, I made conditions that I was sure they would not accept. To my surprise, they accepted them all, even a constitutional change. "Gentlemen, there remains a big hurdle. I must sell the house where I live and that seems impossible."

"Oh, that is nothing," the men replied, "we will pray and God will sell it."

I thought, "Well, that's what you think. We have prayed three years to sell it without result." But sure enough, the week we returned to St. Louis there was an offer to purchase.

We moved to Chicago in 1950 to the most active, growing, aggressive church I had ever pastored. The work of the church was done by committees, and chairmen did not hesitate to make decisions.

One day, feeling like a fifth wheel, I wrote my resignation and gave it to the treasurer, whom I had come to know best of all the leaders. He read it and said, "Pastor, have you gone out of your mind?"

"Well, maybe."

"What's wrong?"

"Oh, this church doesn't need me."

"Pastor, we didn't invite you here to be the janitor, or to paint the place, or even to run errands. You are our pilot, the spark plug to inspire us. I'll hold your resignation secretly for six months. If at the end of that time you are not convinced that this is the most spiritual group of people you have ever had, that we are a most loving church family and that we are winning more souls than any other congregation you ever had, then I'll submit your resignation."

Nothing further was ever said about the matter.

Every Friday night was given over to visitation. I found one big difficulty though. The people on whom I called were watching TV and many times did not turn it off or even down. One Friday night I came home thoroughly disgusted. Television had won the battle of the evening. "Dorothy, I'm disgusted. Television is ruining the greatest program of this church. If people won't listen to me when I'm in their homes, I'll make them listen to me on television."

So I went to the most influential television station in Chicago and asked to see the manager, who was also the owner.

"Yes, send the preacher in," he told his secretary.

"What do you want?"

Boldly I stated, "I would like to go on television on Sunday in prime time."

"Do you know what that would cost in a city this size?"

"No."

"Nine hundred dollars for one full half-hour."

For a moment I was speechless. "Sir, if I feel I can make it, what chance would I have to go on?"

"Let me ask you three questions. Would you ever preach on hell on television?"

I thought, here goes my chance if I ever had one at all. "Yes, sir, there is a fair chance I just might do that because I believe hell is just as real as heaven and everyone is going to one or the other."

"Would you appeal for funds on your program?"

"Yes, I would, but I trust it would be in good taste."

"What kind of financial backing would you have?"

"Only my faith in God who keeps His promises as

given in the Bible."

"Son, you can go on."

I almost fainted.

He continued, "You see, I'm the son of an old-fashioned Methodist preacher. I think hell fire needs to be preached. I also know a church organization has to appeal for funds. As to the third question, if you have that much faith in God, I'll trust you to pay your bill. When do you wish to start?"

To the best of my investigative knowledge, ours was the first television program sponsored by a local church on a regular basis in any metropolitan area. It certainly was the first one in Chicago.

With prop costs, cost of talent and other normal expenses, it averaged over $1,100 per program.

The response was excellent. One week we received 1,350 letters, the largest single response the station had had up to that time. Many found Christ as their Savior during the six-month television series.

The church consistently grew the five years I was there as pastor, but in the last six months I began to feel the great burden for the city lift. I had accomplished the 15 projects the Lord had laid on my heart as pastor of Jefferson Park Bible Church.

I began to feel an inward pressure to enter the field of evangelism. More and more invitations came to hold evangelistic meetings. At the same time, I really didn't want to give up the fruits of my labor—a full congregation, the best financial situation I had ever had, and being known in a large city like Chicago. Evangelism would not furnish sufficient remuneration to keep my children in college. I did not want to leave my family. I still had a son, who would be spending four years in high school mostly without his dad. Nor did I like the sense of insecurity. As an evangelist, nobody would be responsible to me or for me.

As I resisted the impressions of the Holy Spirit, He, in turn, let me know in various ways that evangelism was God's will for me.

Finally, one morning in my study, in desperation I said to God, "If You will show me from the Scriptures that I should be an evangelist, I will resign." I felt sure I had solved my inner urgings.

For two weeks I had peace of heart and mind. Then one day at family worship, our portion was Numbers 8. When it was my turn, I began to read:

> "This is it that belongeth unto the Levites: from twenty and five years old and upward they shall go in to wait upon the service of the tabernacle of the congregation: And from the age of fifty years they shall cease waiting upon the service thereof, and shall serve no more: But rather shall minister with their brethren. . . ."

God had given me an answer from His Word. I had just celebrated my 50th birthday about a week before. Dorothy and I prayed together for God's will and I typed out my resignation, effective in 60 days.

It was also while I was pastor in Chicago that John Brown University conferred upon me an honorary doctor of divinity degree, stating that it was bestowed in recognition of my pioneer efforts in Youth for Christ and subsequent work among the youth of our nation, and also for being the first pastor to have a regular weekly telecast in a metropolitan city.

If any of you lack wisdom, let him ask of God, who giveth to all men liberally, and upbraideth not, and it shall be given him.

James 1:5

26 If She Blows, Let 'er Blow!

To describe the events involved in the five years of preaching and crisscrossing America in campaigns and crusades is beyond the scope of this book.

My mandate was the declaration of the gospel and my constant goal the winning of souls. Besides the actual evangelistic preaching, I did some church growth consultation in churches that requested it.

I also learned many interesting things: the ratio for chicken, turkey and roast beef dinners which I was served was 27-2-2 respectively! I discovered too that the Apostle Paul and I had very much in common—he was beaten but I was jabbed all night in some of the most horrendous beds imaginable!

Nevertheless, God honored the five years of evangelistic ministry with much fruit that remains to this day. It was the proof of my calling as an evangelist.

But toward the end of those five years, a Canadian church invited me for an interim ministry of 18 months. And barring my election as superintendent of the Southeastern District of The Christian and Missionary Alliance, which I considered unlikely, I was inclined to go. My wife and I made plans to move from Florida to Toronto, Canada.

At the time of the election in the Southeastern District, I was ministering at another conference. A phone call came Friday morning, "We are calling to inform you that you have been elected superintendent of the Southeastern District."

"Thank you." I hung up the phone and sat down and wept. I hadn't realized how much I had counted on the respite of settling down and being at home for at least a year.

I phoned my wife to tell her the news. She was also disappointed. In addition she said, "What do you know about being a district superintendent?"

"Nothing."

"I don't think this is your cup of tea."

"Yes, I know, but I'm in it regardless."

Being a superintendent was a new kind of life for which I had neither training nor experience. Nor did I feel I had the natural equipment for administration.

The first three or four months, if there had been a convenient or legitimate way out, I would have taken it.

It seemed that every night, between 10:00 and midnight, I would receive from three to eight telephone calls from pastors wanting immediate solutions to their problems, or church boards wanting action from the district superintendent. I began to think that everyone had waited until the new superintendent was elected so that they could dump their built-in difficulties into his lap.

In response to these calls, I gave my considered opinions and then lay awake the rest of the night wondering if what I had said was right. If my replies were wrong, their churches might go to pieces. A few weeks of this and I felt I was headed for a nervous breakdown. I would have gladly given the job to anyone.

I took a day off, went down to the seashore and walked along the beach, praying, thinking, trying to get quiet enough to hear God's voice. I was desperate. "Oh God, you must give me the equipment I need for this job. I didn't seek it, nor do I really want it. All I want is your will."

"My child," He seemed to whisper to me, "I have promised to supply all your needs. 'If any man lacks wisdom, let him ask of me. I give liberally.' " How the thought of an overflowing amount was emphasized to me!

"Thank you, Jesus." Then I prayed, "Lord, this will be my procedure. I will give the advice and answers I feel are the best according to my judgment. If my solutions are wrong, it is Your fault, not mine, for I am willing to tell them anything You tell me. My complete trust is in You for the right answers. If the Southeastern District blows, let 'er blow! It is Your district, the churches are Yours and the pastors are Your shepherds."

The sweetest peace swept over me. All anxiety was gone. Worry disappeared and a new confidence flooded my whole being. My heart and mind were truly at rest. I believe the Holy Spirit gave to me at that time the gift of administration.

One day I received a phone call from the acting chairman of a church board.

"Mr. Harvey, we have called such and such a man as pastor of our church."

Just a few days prior to this I had received information that under this man's ministry there had been several church fights and congregational splits. The church from which the call had just come was not that homogenous, and I knew it could not survive that kind of pastor.

"You cannot have him," I answered.

"But he has already been called." (This procedure was contrary to the rules of our society.) "He is our pastor."

"You still can't have him . . . The moment he enters your pulpit as your pastor, you cease to be a Christian and Missionary Alliance Church."

"You can't do that," the chairman retorted.

"Try me and see. I'll write that church off the records. That's final." And I hung up.

My wife heard my emphatic tone of voice. She was frightened.

"Can you do that?"

"I have already done it," was all I could answer.

I went apart to pray. "Lord, I have taken drastic action and believe it is the correct thing to do. It is Your problem."

The chairman was at the boiling point. Anger seemed almost a mild word. But he knew I meant what I said. The church board didn't call the man. They called instead the man I had recommended. He became a most successful and God-blessed man to them and the church experienced the largest growth in its history under his ministry.

On another occasion, five men appeared at the close of a service. The spokesman, without any introduction, began speaking. "Sir, next Sunday we are going to call Mr. _____ as our pastor whether you approve or not." (The man to whom he referred was a complete stranger to me.)

"Apparently you are not familiar with our procedure in calling a pastor," I said as softly as I could. "We are not adverse to a man outside our society. However, there is a method we follow which protects the prospective pastor as well as the church from making an unfortunate choice."

The spokesman did not wait for further explanation, but raised his arm and shook his fist under my nose. "I want you, Mr. Superintendent, to understand that we have come only to notify you that we are calling this man."

Ignoring the man's aggressive gestures, I continued to speak in a controlled voice. "Our method is for two members of the district executive committee to sit down with the candidate and attempt to evaluate the man's educational background, spiritual experience and call to preach."

"He's not going to meet with anybody, nor is anybody from any committee going to talk with him."

As nicely as I knew how, I tried to explain how it could be done.

"But," he continued, "we are not sending him to anybody and nobody is meeting with him. Do you understand that this is final?"

With anger in his voice he shook his fist so close that sometimes he touched my nose.

"I want you to understand that next Sunday at 3:00 this board is going to call Mr. _____ as our pastor, and there is nothing you or anybody else can do about it."

"I am very sorry, sir, that you will not listen to reason nor try to understand our procedure. I have recourse that you probably cannot understand."

I walked away and went to my room to pray.

"Lord Jesus, I have done everything I know to do. It would appear that this man is going to rule or ruin and probably both. I turn him over to You completely and take my hands off."

I had peace of mind and went to sleep.

Apparently, over my objections, the meeting was held the next Sunday. But about 3:30 p.m., the phone rang. I was wakened from a Sunday afternoon nap. A woman's voice, interspersed with sobs, said, "Reverend Harvey, my husband just dropped dead. He wouldn't do what was right. I'm Mrs. _____."

The news spread throughout the district. I heard men say, "Don't oppose Harvey, you might get into trouble."

The Lord's promise to me was, "The Lord shall fight for you and ye shall hold your peace" (Exodus

14:14).

A new confidence that God was directing the superintendency swept through the district. I can assure you, it made my job easier.

At the next district conference I was elected with but two dissenting votes to another three-year term.

*And we know that all things work together for good
to them that love God, to them who are the called
according to his purpose.*

Romans 8:28

27 Detour to Texas

Three years later I found myself without a job
and with a wife who had an incurable disease,
emphysema.

I had resigned the superintendency of the
Southeastern District and had agreed to become the
district superintendent of a new district being
formed in New York. However, that plan was vetoed
by the doctor's verdict that my wife would be dead
in two years if we took up residence there.

Dorothy and I talked about our future and the
possibilities open to us. I was fairly well known in
the evangelistic field. The Lord had always blessed
with visible results and the churches had been
helped. Evangelism also had the advantage
geographically—we could live anywhere in the
United States that we chose and make it our
headquarters.

The doctor who diagnosed Dorothy's case
mentioned the far west, especially Arizona. Our
plans began to focus on that direction.

But during a December business session of the Board of Managers, the president of our society turned to me without any prior conversation and said, "Mr. Harvey, we have no district superintendent in Texas. Would you be willing to be the board's representative in that area?"

"I see no reason why not. I have no definite plans." On December 26th we landed, furniture and all, in Dallas, Texas. We found the beautiful district parsonage much more to our liking than any home we had ever lived in. God was surely doing the "exceedingly abundant" for us.

My wife's first trip to the doctor was not encouraging. He confirmed that Dorothy was well advanced in the disease and maintained there was absolutely no cure for it. There was a possibility of arresting emphysema and bringing some relief with the use of an inhalator, but that was all.

But God gave my wife a promise from His Word, that just as Jesus healed Peter's wife's mother and she arose and ministered to Jesus and the disciples (Matthew 8:14–15), so He would do for her, that she could perform all the responsibilities that might be hers as the wife of a district superintendent.

God did just that. In fact, she entertained more than ever before, even with the difficulty in breathing.

For two years she went every six months for an examination. One day, her physician asked, "Mrs. Harvey, what medication am I giving you?"

"None."

"What treatment?"

"None, except using the inhalator a half hour a day as you prescribed."

"That's no cure, that is only to make you more comfortable. You need not return for a year."

Each year of the eight we lived in Dallas, she returned for an examination. Each year the X-rays showed less of the disease until Dr. Schools would exclaim, "These are amazing!"

Later the doctor who examined Dorothy for missionary service said, "If Dr. Schools had not so affirmed, I would say you never had emphysema, as there is no evidence of it at all."

Praise God, He had performed another miracle! Gradually, but perfectly.

For as many as are led by the Spirit of God, they are the sons of God.

Romans 8:14

28 LeTourneau College

I was delighted when I was asked to serve on the board of trustees of LeTourneau College, Longview, Texas. Richard LeTourneau, the president of the college, had meant much to me and the Southwestern District through his wise counseling. I felt the invitation would give me the opportunity to at least show a little appreciation. (LeTourneau College is a Christian college. At that time it had several hundred students who specialized in engineering, but it also has departments of liberal arts, business and religion.)

One day at a specially called meeting of the board, Richard informed the trustees that because of his father's ill health he had no choice but to assume the leadership of the LeTourneau Corporation and that someone else would have to be appointed to take the responsibility for the college.

A nominating committee was appointed. Its nominee was Richard Harvey. I was stunned.

My reaction was instantaneous. "I can't, gentlemen. This is not my field nor experience.

Besides, this is largely a technical school and I know nothing about engineering. I have a job, too, from which I can't conscientiously resign because no one can be elected to take my place before next fall, a year from now."

All my speeches were ignored. I was decreed elected and Richard LeTourneau and Richard Harvey were to work out the difficulties.

After consultation with our denominational officials in New York, it was determined that for one year I would maintain both positions, that of district superintendent and of executive vice-president of LeTourneau College and that we would live in Longview. Thus from Monday morning until Friday noon, I served the college. On Friday afternoon the college furnished a plane and pilot and on Friday evening, Saturday and Sunday I served the district. Every evening after 10:00 I called my secretary in Dallas, the mail was read to me and answers were dictated over the phone.

A book could be written on the marvelous ways God gave wisdom and worked for me at the college. My title was Executive Vice-President, with full responsibility for operating the college. The wisdom, ideas, favor and guidance the Lord gave were outstanding.

One day one of the administrative staff, who certainly would never have voted in my favor had he had an opportunity, came to my office. "Dr. Harvey, I want to ask forgiveness for making it difficult for you. I am positive now that God is with you and blessing you and I am not going to have any part in opposing the Lord's work."

The illustration is but one of the many I could give of divine intervention on my behalf.

I had been at LeTourneau College only a couple of weeks when there was a breathing spell at the office. I reached for some of the books in the pile on my desk which Richard LeTourneau had put there that I might familiarize myself with many aspects of college administration.

I scanned a few until I came to a little book entitled *The Organization of America's Small Colleges and Universities*. On the first page was a list of those who were members: our college was listed.

I thought, "I'd better discover what the organization is all about." So I fingered through the pages with one thought, "I'll return to this when I have more time."

I laid the book aside. But a strong impression came over me to pick it up again. I have learned to obey the "inner voice of the Spirit."

About one-third of the way through was a picture of the organization's full-time director. I read the caption under the picture, then began to thumb through the pages again.

The impression came again, "Look at the picture. Read the caption carefully." I did.

Again, "Read it carefully."

Again I read it carefully, and laid the book down.

Then there was a knock on my office door—a man had come directly, not through the secretary. When I saw him, I responded, "Good morning, Dr. _____."

"How do you know me?" (He almost lost his balance standing there.) "You have never seen me before, have you?"

"No, I have never met you either. Sir, I don't think you would understand if I tried to explain."

"You're new here, aren't you?"

"Yes, sir, I am pinch-hitting for Richard LeTourneau."

"But I want to know how you knew who I was. No one knew I was coming here. I didn't know myself until I was flying over Longview and decided to stop for a few minutes. I met no one on the journey or on the campus."

I saw I was going to have to give an explanation.

"Just before you came in, sir, I was talking to God and seeking guidance for the day. An inner urge led me to read your little book on America's small colleges and universities."

"Oh, so you're one of those religious crackpots."

"Yes, sir, I'm in that classification." I explained how I was led to pick up the little book after laying it aside. I told him how God had stopped me at his picture and how He had guided me to reread the paragraph under the picture. I then quoted it practically word for word.

"You must be one of those religious fanatics like my daughter. She got religion at one of Billy Graham's meetings."

"Yes, sir, that is exactly the same thing I have. Both your daughter and I have the same Christ."

The incident seemed to keep him from leaving. He hung around all day. We went to lunch together.

Before the day was over, I had prayed with him. He left with his eyes full of tears. His parting words were, "Dr. Harvey, I'm convinced there must be something real to this religious bit."

> *. . . Go ye into all the world, and preach the gospel to every creature.*

> **Mark 16:15**

29 Missionaries at Last!

In 1960 we began a series of missionary ministries that has taken us overseas various times and around the world more than once. Included in these most fruitful years of our lives was a three-year appointment to World Evangelism (1972–1974) by our own mission.

To enumerate the countries visited is not necessary. And to fully chronicle these harvest years would require a dozen books.

But there have been some experiences that belong in these pages. In what might, for some, be called retirement years, we have seen the Holy Spirit work as He did in the book of Acts.

It began with a work of God's provision for my wife.

I had been invited to be the speaker at a missionary conference in West Africa. Missionaries would be coming from Upper Volta, Mali, Guinea and Ivory Coast.

As I made plans to go, my wife said, "Don't count on my going with you as the cost would be

171

prohibitive." But I knew she wanted to see our missionary sons, one in Tangiers, Morocco, and the other in Guinea.

"Let us pray and trust God for the ticket," I suggested.

"No, I don't feel free to ask the Lord to put it on someone's heart; it might be that folks would take it from giving to some missionary or gospel project, and it is not a must that I go."

"But remember, God is not tied to our resources," I remonstrated.

A few weeks later, Dorothy received a letter from an attorney in Ohio asking if she were related to a Mable Kress, an aunt who had been dead for some time. The attorney stated that in the will there was one piece of property, a farm that had her aunt's name on the deed. The court had decreed that one-sixteenth of the sale of the farm was Dorothy's. It proved to be sufficient to pay for her ticket.

I have often thought that her uncle, who had no religious faith at all, would have "turned over in his grave" if he had known that his niece was using his money to tour mission fields.

It was just another miracle of God's provision.

Soon after arriving back in America after a much blessed trip to Zaire in 1969, invitations began to come from our mission fields in Asia. To each I replied that the invitation had been received and appreciated, and that I would pray about the matter.

At a committee meeting at our headquarters, the vice-president in charge of foreign missions said to me, "Harvey, what are you going to do about those invitations from the Far East? You can't just write them polite answers. They need to know yes or no."

"All right, Dr. King, let me ask you a definite question. Do you personally want me to go?"

"Yes, I do."

"All right, I'll plan to go and you will hear from me soon as to what I feel is the best time."

Later, someone asked me, "How are you going to finance your trip?"

"I suppose the same way I always have. I'll pray to God and He will send it in."

"I am a member of a foundation that I think would help if you would write and request assistance."

"I have never asked for money for myself in my life, and I do not think I am ready to start now."

"This is different," my friend said. "I am asking you to request the grant."

"Let me pray about it."

At the next meeting of the Board of Trustees of LeTourneau College, one of the committee members who knew about the matter asked, "Have you written yet requesting the grant?"

"No, I haven't."

"It is probably a good thing. There is a new federal ruling for foundations that states that no gifts can be given to individuals. The request must come from an organization registered with the Internal Revenue Service as a bona fide charity. Why don't you have one of your denominational officers write the letter?"

"Give me a couple of days to think that one over," I said. I needed to receive guidance from God in order to make a proper decision. I prayed, "Lord, if I am hesitant because of pride and this is what you want me to do, have my path cross that of one of your officials." In two days I unexpectedly met our vice-president, Dr. L. L. King. I told him of the conversation at the trustees' meeting. His reaction was gratifying.

"I'll be delighted to write the letter."

He must have done it almost immediately. Within a week I received a grant sufficient to pay for my tickets from country to country on a trip that would take a full year.

Thus at the next Board of Managers' meeting in New York, the report from the Foreign Department asked for the appointment of Dr. and Mrs. Richard Harvey as missionaries for World Evangelism for one year, provided their physical examinations were satisfactory. That appointment was later extended for two more years.

I phoned Dorothy from New York to tell her of the board's affirmative vote. Her immediate response was, "Well, after 43 years we are finally appointed to be missionaries! You know, if I had known that we were not going to be missionaries, I would never have married you. But it's working out wonderfully well."

Then there was the hurdle of the physical examinations. When I took the examination the doctor said, "Reverend, you will have to have surgery before I can recommend you for this foreign travel." So the surgery was scheduled.

When Dorothy was examined the doctor said,

"Mrs. Harvey, I am giving you a clean bill of health. I am noting here on the record that you have no emphysema." At the conclusion of his report, he wrote, "I find no reason why Mrs. Harvey cannot go to any place she might travel or fulfill any assignment that may be given her."

After accepting the assignment for this one year of evangelistic ministry around the world, we discovered that the cost was much greater than we had first anticipated. Dorothy suggested that to economize, she should spend part of the time in Australia with our youngest son.

But God reminded me of the many times I had said, "God is not poor and the Bible teaches that giving does not impoverish Him and withholding doesn't make Him rich. He still has other ravens than those that fed Elijah." I asked for God's forgiveness and arranged for Dorothy's ticket.

Just before the tickets were to be paid, the Southwestern District gave us a testimonial farewell dinner in Dallas, Texas. Near the close of the lovely affair, the master of ceremonies, Dr. Harry Hardwick, called my wife to the podium and presented her with a box. She was first asked to read a poem especially written for her:

Man alone, forbid the thought!
The Word has said, good it is not.
Our thoughts and prayers will follow you
And gifts that wife may follow too.

She was then asked to open the box and count the money. There was $2,100 in one-dollar bills. "Now," they said, "your ticket will be at least

$2,500. In the next month you will receive the balance." And she did.

And ye shall seek me, and find me, when ye shall search for me with all your heart.

Jeremiah 29:13

30 The Seeker

In Upper Volta I met one of the most unforgettable characters I have ever encountered. The missionary in whose home I stayed the first night said, "Harvey, there is a tribesman in this country you ought to meet."

"Well, let's meet him."

"Oh, it's not that easy. He lives a full day's journey from here. The roads are rough and he might not even be alive. He is very aged and I have not heard from him in many months."

"By the way you talk, it makes me want to take the chance. Can we go tomorrow?"

As we traveled, the missionary told me the man's story.

When he was 21, he sent for the village elders and they met in front of the palaver hut. He took his bag of religious paraphernalia and dumped it out on the ground along with his many fetishes.

"I have no confidence in any of these. There is Somebody up there (pointing to the sky) who made the sun, moon, stars, trees and animals. And He

177

made me, and I want to worship Him. No one has told me about Him, but I am sure He is up there."

Thus for 10 years every morning at sunrise, the young man went out in the tall grass outside the village, lifted his eyes toward the heavens and with his arms upraised cried out, "Oh You, up there, whoever You are, I worship You."

After 10 years of daily praying and seeking, a Moslem teacher heard about him and came to live with him. The teacher told him about Allah and read the Koran to him.

Then one day, very abruptly, he turned to the teacher and said, "You can leave. This Allah you are telling me about is not the Man in the sky I am praying to."

Every day for many more years, this man continued to pray each morning. "Oh You, up there, whoever You are, make Yourself known to me; I want to worship You."

A Catholic priest heard about this man who prayed so faithfully, so he came to live with him and teach him. He told him about the God of the Bible, about God sending His son Jesus Christ and about Christ's death on the cross as payment for our sins. After a little more than two weeks, the man said to the priest, "The story you tell about your God of the sky and His son Jesus being sent into the world sounds sweet and I like the words of the Book you read to me. Somehow I believe it might be true, but you can go now. I don't like the things you do, things I would not do if I believed in the Man of the Book as you say you do."

So the priest went away.

More than five years passed. Finally, a missionary was told about the man in the distant town. He went to inquire and found him easily because the man was well known.

The missionary read from the same Book as had the priest. As he did so, the man's face lit up. "I've heard that Book before." The missionary told him the story of Christ's death and resurrection.

"Oh, this Man in the skies is alive now?"

"Yes," and the missionary went on to explain His ascension and promised return. In a matter of only a few days the seeker of many years had opened his life to Jesus Christ.

When I saw him, he was very old. His hair was as white as snow. The wrinkles in his face were so deep that one might place his fingers in the furrows. His aged eyes could only distinguish light from darkness. Every morning his wife placed him outside their mud hut on a mat with only a roof of grass and banana leaves to shelter him from the hot African sun.

When we arrived and the missionary spoke his name, his face lit up. The old man recognized the missionary's voice. After they had conversed briefly, he reached up and took a piece of paper from under the thatched roof. It was old and worn. It was a page from the New Testament. He proceeded to quote it and then returned it to its place. He then found another sheet of paper and rubbed his hand over that—it was from a songbook. Then he tried to sing the song in his quavery, cracked voice.

Before we left, his head turned in the direction of the missionary's voice, and he asked, "Teacher, would you have that young man come close to me?" (I felt honored—I was in my fifties.) He reached out to find my body and kept feeling until he found my arm, then my wrist. He pulled me to the ground beside him.

Feeling around until his hands found the top of my head, he began to pray. I've had many pray for me down through the years, great men of God, but never have I felt God's power so real as when this elderly African saint prayed for me. There seemed to be a current flowing from his body into mine.

"And ye shall seek me and find me when ye shall search for me with all your heart" (Jeremiah 29:13).

I had met an African who had sought against tremendous odds.

And he had found!

*And let us not be weary in well doing; for in due
season we shall reap if we faint not.*

Galatians 6:9

31 Payoffs Everywhere!

There have been a lot of delightful little "payoffs"
along the way in my service for Christ. One of them
came in Ecuador.

Some missionaries from the Wycliffe Bible
Translators had taken me to a building filled with
computers where they demonstrated how a totally
new language is translated into sounds. I was
introduced to the young man in charge who
explained the complete process to me. I'll admit it
was very complex. I thanked him and started down
the path to the mission headquarters.

I had gone only two or three hundred yards when
I heard someone coming behind me. I turned to see
the young fellow who had just explained the
equipment. He was now coming down the path on a
bicycle! When he reached me he slammed on the
brakes and excitedly said, "Are you the Dick Harvey
from St. Louis?"

"Yes, I lived in St. Louis for nine years."

"Would you believe it? I am here because of you. I
was a soldier at Scott Field during the war. I was

saved at one of your Youth for Christ rallies and dedicated my life to the Lord there too. Once when a missionary spoke, God created the desire in my heart to be a missionary."

He jumped off his bike and hugged me. It was some payoff, believe me!

In Canberra, Australia, I was scheduled to hold an evangelistic campaign in my son John's church.

"Dad," he said, "I want you to open your campaign with a sermon on healing."

"Well, I do not object to preaching once on healing in any campaign, but to open the series with that sort of sermon is a new experience for me," I replied.

"Dad, I want you to open with a sermon on healing!"

I brought the sermon on healing. Among the responses, two cases stand out in my memory.

A young married woman who had been born with one leg a few inches shorter than the other requested prayer. She had never known even a few hours free from pain. When she was prayed for, the pain ceased, and an operation that was scheduled was canceled.

The next day her mother, who was of another faith, came to help her with the housework and noticed that her daughter did not need to rest every few moments as usual. The mother had been very angry at her daughter for attending the church my son pastored.

The next Sunday the mother came with her daughter to the service and in the middle of the meeting interrupted, "Pastor, I've got to ask God and you to forgive me." She told about the healing of her daughter. She herself became a Christian. At last report, the girl's leg that was too short was gradually growing longer.

Then there was the case of a splendid young couple. They had heard of the miracles, and so one day they came to us.

"We have no children. We are like Abraham and Sarah in the Bible. Our doctors say we can never have a child. Do you think God could perform a miracle for us?"

"Yes. He has done it for many down through the centuries."

"Would you pray for us?"

We did of course, and in due time, after we had returned to the States, we received a birth announcement from the joyful couple.

Our next assignment was a month in the Philippines. In Manila, I had a daily speaking assignment at various luncheons. Unknown to me, one of the engagements was at a political club.

Although I was the speaker for the day, I was not placed next to the master of ceremonies, but next to the auxiliary bishop of the Roman Catholic church in the Manila area. We chatted amiably.

I was disturbed as to what I should speak about to that type of audience. I could not decide, nor did the Holy Spirit give me direction until I rose to speak. The impression inside was then very clear, "Tell the people how they can find Jesus Christ and how they can know Him personally for themselves."

As I cast my eyes over the audience it seemed that the most appreciative and attentive listener was the bishop. Soon I noticed him wiping tears from his eyes.

When I finished speaking and returned to my seat, the auxiliary bishop reached under the table to find my hand. He squeezed it so hard I thought he would break the bones. In fact, my hand hurt for three days afterward! The tears began to flow down his face; he made no attempt to wipe them away.

"Sir, this is the greatest day of my life. I joined the priesthood because of a sincere desire to know God. Today I have found Him. I have peace, peace. Sir, this is the greatest day of my life."

We shed many tears of joy together.

The voice of the Lord is upon the waters. The God of Glory thundereth; the Lord is upon many waters.

Psalm 29:3

32 Revival in Indonesia

In the city of Makassar, Indonesia, we visited the Jaffray School of Theology. I was given extended chapel services each day to minister to the students. One morning the Holy Spirit broke in upon us. A student stood in the service and asked to speak. "I can't hold this any longer," he said. Then he broke forth in public confession of his sins. When he finished another stood and on and on it went, until I believe every student had publicly confessed his sins.

In mid-afternoon, the missionaries, feeling the service had gone long enough, closed the meeting. But the next day during class periods, the confessions began again. The missionaries sensed that the Holy Spirit was truly at work because of the heartfelt confessions and restitutions which marked the meetings.

On the small island of Roti, Indonesia, God gave me one of the most unusual ministries of my life. Roti had been touched by a gospel team from the revival on the neighboring island of Timor. The people had seen God mightily display His power through the team's witness.

My invitation to Roti had been extended by the head of the Dutch Reformed Church in that section of the island chain. He had invited 13 churches from half of the island to gather in an open field. There were over 2,500 present by actual count.

The invitation to accept Christ was the most carefully phrased appeal I had ever given in my 45 years of ministry. When I concluded the uncompromising declaration of the cost of following Christ, I said to the people seated on the ground, "You who sincerely want to invite Christ into your lives, you who will confess your sins and forsake them, you who will give up all your fetish worship and sorcery, please stand." Like a trained choir all but 43 people stood to their feet. I turned to the missionary. "They did not understand or they are just trying to please me."

"No. I'll explain later. Just counsel with them en masse as you have done elsewhere."

Afterward, my missionary escort explained that this massive response was the result of two unusual factors: first, the pastors, all 13 of them, had recently come to a vital and personal knowledge of Christ. Second, there was an intense desire in the area to know Christ because of the powerful witness of the gospel team from Timor.

At Jayapura, the capital of Irian Jaya, I was speaking nightly and one evening in the service a very strong impression came to me. It was a strong inner voice, so strong that I paused to see if the audience was hearing also.

"At the close of the services, tell that young man in the front seat that you will come to his area for meetings."

I tried to argue with God in the pause that one always has with an interpreter, but I found myself getting confused in my preaching. In order to get relief from the pressure of the inner voice I said, "All right God, I will tell him after the service."

Afterward, I asked a missionary to introduce me to the young man. He said, "This is Franz Selan, the brother-in-law of Mel Tari, who wrote the book *Like a Mighty Wind*."

"It is a pleasure to meet you. God told me to tell you that I should come and speak for you."

"Oh, I know that."

I was taken aback because only a few minutes before I had told God I would go.

"I will come next Tuesday and Wednesday."

"I have benches and a loudspeaker already rented for that time. You are already advertised. I asked Mr. Catto, the mission chairman, to have you come to us for meetings. But he said you were booked up. So I went to God. I asked for His forgiveness for asking man and then I asked my Heavenly Father to send you to me. He told me He would. He also showed me the field I was to obtain and how many benches to rent and the time for the meetings. We are all prepared and the whole city of Abapura (the only university city of Irian Jaya) knows you are coming."

I said to the missionary, "Who is that young

preacher anyway?"

"Don't you know him? Hasn't anybody told you about him?"

"No."

"Well, he is the young man through whom the Holy Spirit flowed in the great miracles of Timor."

I could hardly wait to see what God would do when Tuesday came. At the very first service all the seats were filled, with about the same number standing. At the end of the message, 104 persons lined up in response to the invitation to find Christ. They were taken one by one into Franz' house to be dealt with and brought to the Savior. Ninety-one of these were men—college professors, heads of the Department of Education, business and professional men.

The next service was much like the first, only this time mostly women responded, the wives of the men who had come the night before. Many outstanding events happened in that visit. It was a confirmation to me that the Timor revival was truly of God. The Holy Spirit was still performing miracles through the same human instrument.

And these signs shall follow those who believe; in my name shall they cast out demons. . . .

Mark 16:17

33 Demons in Gabon

In Gabon we saw an outstanding example of the deliverance Christ can bring to a person who is possessed by demons.

The victim's name was Edward. He was a young man, highly educated by Gabonese standards, and the superintendent of that nation's second largest school system.

Edward's troubles began when he became angry at his school board (which was directed by an American mission) for rejecting his request for some desired equipment. Refusing to accept the board's explanation, Edward became bitter, resigned all his church responsibilities and eventually ceased to attend services. He also became sick.

Whatever his sickness was, he grew worse. He visited the community doctor, but the doctor could not help him. Edward then went to Libreville to the large government hospital. They could do nothing for him either.

He was forced to resign his position with the schools. Edward's parents, who were pagans, pressured him into taking a fetish. He took it and hid it secretly. Soon he became involved in former heathen practices and living as he had before he became a Christian. One day he went to a nearby village and secretly took a second wife, but let her remain in the village with her tribe. His health continued to deteriorate and it soon was evident that he had gone insane. The Christian leaders all pronounced him demon possessed.

One day Edward seemed to be rational for a few hours. He called his wife, who had remained true to God and to him during this terrible time, and explained to her all the things he had done, confessing his sin and adultery. He said to her, "I don't want to die with all these sins on my heart. Will you pray that God will heal me long enough that I can make things right before I die?" They prayed together and he confessed his sins to Christ and sought forgiveness. But Edward went back into that terrible state of insanity.

After a couple of days he awoke, quite normal and immediately started out to fulfill his promises to God. He asked forgiveness of many he had wronged, restored some things he had stolen, returned to the village where he had the second wife and released her, satisfying both her and her parents according to their custom. Then he returned to his former state of insanity—only worse than before. His body grew weaker and his ravings increased.

One day in a rational moment, he called his wife to his side. "I believe God has accepted me, but if you could get some ministers, men of God who have faith, to come and pray for me, I believe God would heal me."

The very next day the missionary and I drove into the village where Edward lived. The same day, the pastor of the local church returned from his vacation and the district's national evangelist also arrived in town unexpectedly. Four ministers in town at the same time was most unusual, but God was arranging it all.

As soon as Edward's wife heard this, she sent a messenger for the four of us to come to their house on the hill. We learned that Edward's relatives from all over Gabon, including an uncle who was a notorious witch doctor, had come to the home for his death. We suggested that the wife bring Edward to the pastor's hut.

Soon we saw them coming down the hill. Edward was being led like a child. He was a sight—frail, dirty, his hair matted and unkempt, his fingernails like claws, and his eyes staring and wild. His wife sat him on one of the few chairs in the hut and stood by his side with her hand on his shoulder to keep him under control.

We had a session of prayer for ourselves, asking God to cleanse our hearts from all sin, known and unknown.

The missionary said, "Mr. Harvey, the pastor and evangelist wish you would direct the procedure."

From past experience I knew that singing is many times helpful in deliverance from demon possession. I also knew that there are certain songs that demons abhor—songs of praise to God, songs about the blood of Christ and songs about the name of Jesus. As we sang, Edward began to foam at the mouth and grew violent. Each of us prayed for him and the demons were commanded to come out. Edward managed to get away from those who were holding him. He slid under the table and lay stiff in the center of the room.

We sang again. He screamed the most horrible scream I have ever heard. Once more in the name of Jesus, I commanded the demons to come out. They did so, but with a struggle that left him as dead. His wife was frightened—she thought he had died.

"Oh no," I said, "he will be all right."

That day I was grateful for every experience I had ever had in casting out demons. Edward soon opened his eyes and crawled out from under the table. His eyes were clear. He stood and raised his hands toward heaven and cried out, "I'm free, I'm free! Thank God, I'm free!"

Then he noticed his wife. He threw his arms around her and hugged and kissed her (a very uncommon practice for an African, as they seldom show affection in public).

Edward then tried to run his hands through his matted hair. He looked himself over. "I need a bath and a haircut. Oh, please excuse me." With his wife he walked up the hill. He returned in about a half hour, so clean I would hardly have known him.

But that was not all. On his return, he asked the pastor to call the village together at the church. It was not necessary—the drums had already spread the news and people came from everywhere.

Edward stood and told his story, asking them for forgiveness and promising to make everything right that he had not settled previously.

Then he noticed the fetishes around his wrist, ankles and neck. "Oh, I must get rid of these or I'll be right back where I was before and this time I'll die." Turning to us he said, "Would you men of God go up to the house with me and pray that I will have the courage to remove these fetishes before my family, my relatives and my uncle, the witch doctor?"

We all went to his home on the hill. The room was large and packed with people who had come for Edward's anticipated funeral. Edward sat down with his feet resting on more fetishes. I asked the evangelist to take charge. He prayed for Edward, thanking God for his deliverance and requesting courage and divine protection.

Edward removed the fetishes one by one from his body and put them in a pile on the floor. Every once in a while he would look toward the evangelist and ask him to pray again. When he had removed the last fetish and put it on the pile, he praised God publicly for his freedom from demon power and for his healing.

The witch doctor spoke up. "Oh, he is not permanently healed. I know he'll be right back where he was. I've seen these temporary deliverances before. But I can tell if he is permanently cured." The witch doctor disappeared through a door into another room. He came out with a handful of something that looked like small nuts. He shook them like one would shake dice and then scattered them on the floor.

The crowd was completely silent. The witch doctor stepped back as if to hear what the scattered pieces were saying to him. He disappeared again through the same door and returned with a basket, turned it upside down and set it on the floor. Then he went into the room and brought out a rooster. He took hold of the rooster's head, put it under its wing, placed the rooster on the basket and then stepped back a few feet to watch.

It seemed like 15 minutes to me but was probably less than 10. The rooster did not move.

"Well," in a firm voice the witch doctor said disgustedly, "Edward is permanently healed; if not, the rooster would have gotten off the basket."

I put my arms around the witch doctor and with a smile said, "You see, sir, our God is more powerful than yours. My God loves you and would gladly be your God if you would come to Him. Witch doctors make wonderful Christians when they really know God's Son Jesus."

The witch doctor grunted something like, "This is no place for me," took his paraphernalia and left.

He has been on my heart many times since then and I trust that someone will be able to win him to Christ. A public evangelistic meeting was held in the village that very night and many turned to the Lord.

It was worth all the heat, bugs and dust just to see God work His wonders in Gabon.

The angel of the Lord encampeth round about those who fear him, and delivereth them.

Psalm 34:7

34 Angel in the Way

Our missionary journeys involved many thousands of miles of travel by every kind of vehicle imaginable. Unnumbered hotels. Strange food and cultures. And the rockets of war.

Through it all, we sensed God's hand of protection and personal care. God's angels, if you like, were watching over us.

For example, in Swaziland where we were to minister to the missionaries of Trans World Radio, our communications got mixed up and there was no one to meet us when we arrived. We could find neither the name of our contact man nor the name of the mission in the telephone book. The immigration officials demanded that we give them an address where we would be staying. I called on God for help.

Just as it looked like we were going to be put on the plane and sent out of the country, my wife spotted a Holiday Inn station wagon. I quickly said to the man, "We will be staying at the Holiday Inn." That was acceptable to him.

We were told by the driver that he doubted that there would be any vacancy as it was the fifth anniversary of their republic and many visitors were coming into the country. We said we would take the chance and the Lord did have a room for us. A cancellation had just been received!

But we still had to contact the mission if we were going to have any ministry. All our efforts seemed in vain.

In desperation we both went to God in prayer. When we arose from our knees, I felt inclined to look in the phone book—one of those inner urges that God's children soon come to recognize as the guidance of the Holy Spirit.

I started down the A's to find some familiar name. When I got to the C's, I found Child Evangelism. I phoned, only to be told that the missionary had moved.

"Could you tell me how I might possibly reach her?"

"Try this number."

I phoned immediately and after five rings a panting voice answered, and I said, "Where can I find the Child Evangelism worker?"

"Oh, I am she, but how did you know to call this number? I don't live here! I just came in to water the plants for my friend. I have been here less than 10 minutes and was just leaving when I heard the phone ringing."

"Well, I am trying to reach the head of Trans World Radio, Dick Olsen. Do you know him?"

"I sure do. In fact, I will be passing his house on

my way home." She delivered the message and within 15 minutes I had a return call.

In an hour my host was there at the motel. A meeting had already been scheduled for the Trans World Radio staff. Other evangelical missionaries had also been invited.

God's timing, as always, was perfect.

After a return visit to Australia, where we had further ministries, we left during their winter months for Vietnam where our mission had ministered for over 50 years. We preached in the midst of war, within the sound of shot and shell. Sometimes we heard a "zing" right over the very building we were in, or sometimes the ground shook beneath our feet as a shell exploded nearby. It was unnerving.

As we saw how calmly the missionaries took it, we too learned to face each day without fear, knowing that God was guarding us just as much in Vietnam as He had in any other place. I found it a sweet experience to realize that nothing can touch God's children without His permission, even in war.

The response to the preaching of the gospel in South Vietnam was tremendous. Sometimes as many as 60% of the audience responded as first-time seekers. Most of those who came forward were young men of military age.

In Phnom Penh, Cambodia, God gave me a great thrill. I saw a Buddhist priest, with shaven head and saffron robe, walk openly down the aisle to confess his sins and turn to Christ. He knew the price he would have to pay to become a follower of Jesus.

The day before he had come to the missionary's home to report his belief in the Christians' God. Holding up a New Testament, he said to Rev. Graven, "I believe this is God's Book and that the God of this Book is the true God. I believe that the story about His son Jesus Christ is true and that He died for my sins. But don't take me wrongly, I am not yet ready to become a Christian—the cost is too great."

Then he continued to explain that before his fellow monks, he would be stripped of his robe, slapped and spat upon and cast bodily out of the monastery. And since no one would receive him, not even his parents, he would die of starvation. So when he came forward that night we knew he had counted the cost.

On our second trip to Cambodia in 1974, I was hit by an auxiliary army ambulance as it came out of the army high command grounds near our mission headquarters. The ambulance swerved to miss a truck and hit me as I walked on the sidewalk by the barbed wire in front of the military establishment.

Normally, I would have been driven by the impact into 15 feet of barbed wire, but contrary to the laws of motion, I was thrown 15 feet parallel to the barbed wire. My shoes were knocked off, one was 20 feet away and the other almost 50 feet.

My watch was picked up nearly 200 feet away by a boy who brought it to me. This was most unusual, as he could just as easily have run with it.

I can never forget how God put His angels around and under me as I was thrown and let down so gently to the ground. I kept hearing the spiritual phrase, "There shall not a bone of him be broken." And to the doctor's surprise and everyone else's, the X-rays showed no broken bones. A miracle indeed!

The first night after this ordeal, when nothing would put me to sleep or kill the pain from the huge bruise on my hip, I wrote the only poem of my life. I was weighing my assets and liabilities.

A war casualty, but no hero.
Discolored, but no purple heart.
Ambulance contact without and within, but
     no stretcher.
Buffeted, pounded, but no broken bones.
Hedged about, but yet tested.
Encircled by angels, yet all alone.
In His hands, yet flying, twisting in mid-air.
Shielded from destruction, but yet so close
     to ruin and disaster.
Private room without a
     hundred-dollar-a-day attachment.
Personal physician, without doctor's bills.
Twenty-four-hour graduate nursing care,
     without charge.
Fourteen X-rays, without Blue Cross or
     Blue Shield.
Hindered, but not thwarted.
Slowed, but not stopped.
Damaged, but not broken.
Detoured, but not sidetracked.

I was black and blue from my knees to my waist and my left arm was swollen twice its normal size at the elbow. I had only a hairline fracture of one rib.

No one could understand it, especially since I was in my late sixties.

But I know the reason. Never before had I sensed the presence of angels like I did when I was flying through the air!

> To the only wise God, our Savior, be glory and
> majesty, dominion and power, both now and ever.
> Amen.

Jude 25

Epilogue

"Sweeter as the years go by" is how the gospel songwriter has expressed it. This has been the story of our lives. God has seen fit to give us a "golden sunset." "The last for which the first was made."

I cannot praise God sufficiently for His goodness to me. He has given me the greatest harvest of a lifetime of ministry in the last five years. Yes, in the past He has always honored my ministry with people finding Christ, but in my sunset years the harvest has been greater still.

Seventy years of God's outstretched hand has been my experience and my ministry does not seem to be over. In my 71st year He is still blessing and performing miracles and giving extended ministries abroad.

While writing these closing words, I am preparing to return to Australia and the Far East for the third time. I will teach 10 weeks in the Alliance College of Theology in Canberra, sharing with the students many of the experiences God has given us. Also,

Dorothy and I will minister at a retreat for pastors and their wives. And so it goes, on and on.

Praise be to God! My heart overflows in thanksgiving to the Father, the Son and the Holy Spirit. "Great things He has done."

Postscript

The event was proving too long for the aging man. Fatigue was plainly written over his features. As we sat together on the platform, he let me know that he wasn't confident he would be able to see it through. He sagged in his chair, waiting to do his part as the graduation speaker for the school for missionaries children in Penang, Malaysia. The date was June 6, 1984. My daughter sat among the graduates, and her grandfather had been chosen to be the guest speaker at her suggestion. In one month he would be 79, and he looked every bit his age.

I recalled how seven years previous Dad and Mom were having an extended ministry with me in Australia and shared the manuscript for the book *Seventy Years of Miracles*. The inner fire that had kept Dad going was still ablaze, though physically he was slowing down. International travel was proving very difficult for a body that was never strong. Nonetheless, he had set a goal to continue in ministry until he was 80. The intervening period was busy with years of evangelistic preaching in North America. However, he had a missionary heart, and the invitation to return to Hong Kong after being at Penang proved irresistible.

A full week of special activities had passed, all part of the build-up to graduation at Dalat, the name this MK school received when previously located in Vietnam. The tropical heat and humidity were draining Dad's energy. Students made a chair of their clasped arms to carry him up and down the long flight of stairs to the dining room by the sea. His walk was labored, his hip and thigh giving him trouble since being hit by an army ambulance in Cambodia in 1974. It looked like the students had invited a has-been as their featured speaker, and even Dad was having his doubts.

The moment for the message arrived, and the inner fire prevailed. The old one spoke to young ones in dynamic tones. The Spirit of God was at work and weakness was being transformed into power. Dad always was at his best when he was weak, so I wasn't surprised to witness once again the perfection of God's strength in Dad's infirmity.

A year later Richard Harvey reached his goal of continuing in ministry until he was 80. True to his word, and sensing it was best for all concerned, he retired to his apartment at Shell Point Village, only leaving it on rare occasions. The next six and a half years were possibly the hardest of his life, fighting pain and a sense of being useless. Nonetheless, a stream of visitors continued to frequent the apartment, most asking for prayer, others for counsel and advice. Mom was his care giver, ever faithful, ministering not only to his physical need but also to his spirit when pain would bring on bouts of depression. In those days prayer flowed from Dad's lips in mighty fervency, revealing that the flame of old had never been diminished. On February 25, 1992, he passed away at the age of 86, his wife and four children and their spouses having waited by his bedside expecting his homegoing. Included among the watching family was the granddaughter who had been part of the graduating class at Dalat, a baby in her arms.

It was a constant wonder to Dad that he who had been born a blue baby, cross-eyed and tongue-tied, should live beyond the Bible's standard of "threescore and ten and if by reason of strength they be fourscore. . . ." While 86 is not in itself especially old, it is for one who knew such severe illness that on three occasions he was pronounced dead. The length of his life was part of the miracle he was experiencing, for it was by reason of strength, God's strength, that he lived so long. I sense it was all part of what the Lord was constantly proving through Richard Harvey's ministry that God was "able to do immeasurably more than all we ask or imagine, according to the power that is at work within us, to Him be the glory in the church and in Christ Jesus throughout all generations, forever and ever! Amen."

John A. Harvey
May 28, 1992
Oxford, England